Armchair Warrior

How a Country Lawyer Learned to Stop Worrying and Love the Law

By John Stonebraker

Peace River Publishing
P.O. Box 1601
Marco Island FL 34145
Copyright © 2012 John Stonebraker
All rights reserved.

ISBN: 0-6156-5472-X
ISBN-13: 9780615654720

Table of Contents

For Mother and Dad

With love, admiration and respect

Me: Mom, in your wildest dreams did you ever think your son would write a book?

Mom: You're not in my wildest dreams.

Acknowledgments

I owe great thanks to my first editor, Michael Garrett. Who knew that "blonde" (with an 'e') only describes *females* with flaxen hair? Michael knows, along with much else. Michael writes and teaches writing as well. His kind words spurred me to continue and persevere to the end. Michael was also Stephen King's first editor. Coincidence? I think not.

My friend and law school classmate, Mark Belz, offered priceless suggestions and wise advice. Mark generously contributed his time and attention to my project, taking precious free time away from his busy law practice and family. Thank you, Mark.

Writing bloggers suggest offering your work to acquaintances whose opinions you value, and who can be depended upon to render objective views. Our friends, Gary and Anne Christensen (former Iowans), Bob and Paulette Kurek and Tony Koduk provided much needed support and encouragement.

Our son, Martin's main suggestion, welcome and carefully considered, but declined, was that I was too hard on judges in my chapter on the judiciary. Notwithstanding, his positive attitude and support were happy by-products of this project.

Finally, my wife, Janelle, read the entire manuscript aloud to me, while we were tucked in bed on our boat at various anchorages off the west coast of Florida. Somehow, the writing flaws jumped out at us better while hearing the spoken word. I'm forever grateful for her support, enthusiasm and endless patience.

Introduction

In 1999 I retired after practicing law in the heartland for thirty years. Our firm grew gradually over that time, and with our growth I discarded other areas of general practice to concentrate on my first love: civil trial work.

While located in a town of around 100,000 in eastern Iowa, I covered mostly rural areas roughly consisting of the eastern one-half of the state from north to south and some parts of western Illinois in state and federal courts for a number of national and regional insurance companies. I was always fully booked with defense assignments; some might say overbooked. My dependable income from defense work allowed me the luxury of picking and choosing a few plaintiffs' cases that came my way.

My criteria for selecting plaintiffs' engagements were twofold. Either the case promised to be particularly rewarding or it presented some serious injustice that I felt needed to be righted. Usually both considerations were present. I never took a plaintiff's case I believed to be wrong. My touchstone was the answer to a simple question I asked myself: would I rather be in the opposing lawyer's shoes or my own? If the answer was that I'd rather be in the other lawyer's shoes, I seldom accepted the case.

On the other hand, I never turned down a defense assignment unless I had a conflict of interest. I would recommend a reasonable settlement in cases where I believed the insured could be found fully or partly to blame for damages caused by his actions, but would try cases where I felt we had an acceptable chance of winning or the terms demanded by the plaintiff were out of reach.

What follows are my memories of selected cases that stand out as interesting and perhaps instructive. Some were winners and some not. Some conflicts resulted in settlements, and some were tried to a conclusion. In all cases I've changed the names of the players. In one case I've also immaterially obscured the underlying facts. While almost all are matters of public record, I choose not to cause any possible embarrassment to former colleagues, clients, opponents, witnesses, or judges.

Iowa calls the document initiating a lawsuit a "Petition." The term most widely used around the country is "Complaint." To conform to the more common usage I've chosen to call the initiating document the "Complaint."

The reader is cautioned that my comments on the law in a particular case are limited to the law of Iowa or Illinois. It may or not be the same as the law of the reader's jurisdiction. Younger readers should remember that my entire professional life took place before GPS, caller ID, computerized legal research and other technological miracles we enjoy today, and take for granted.

Although several of my most significant cases were advanced on behalf of plaintiffs injured in one way or another, I'm sure that a strong defense bias will jump out of the pages. The reader should bear this in mind in thinking through the views and issues presented.

I've reconstructed conversations and snippets of courtroom testimony, opening statements and summations from recollection only. While not word for word, I've tried to accurately capture both the essence and the drama of the moment as closely as memory permits.

I've used the masculine pronouns, he, him and his in all instances to avoid the awkward "he or she" and "him or her." My choice is intended to be gender inclusive. Be assured, dear reader, that I fully understand the political incorrectness of this choice, but I believe a disrupted flow of communication results from the alternative.

Part of my goal in relating these vignettes of my life in the law is to expose and correct some myths about who lawyers are and what they do, admit many faults, and to relate something about how the law really works through the eyes of someone who tried to learn along the way. I'm pleased that my oldest son decided to pursue a legal career, despite lawyer jokes, the largely unfair reputation lawyers endure during their professional lives, the countless weekends his dad spent away from the family, and all the nights he and his younger brother spent fatherless while Dad was on the road.

I'm deeply indebted to my entire family, sons Robert and Martin and my wife of 44 years, Janelle. I don't recall a single time when any of them complained that Dad wasn't around as much as other dads or that he put work ahead of family. My family was then, and is now, my pride and my treasure. I only hope I've served them well by honorable and effective service to the bar, with some measure of balance between these two competitors for my time and energy.

Lawyers often say that the law is a jealous mistress, demanding copious devotion, time, and attention. I ruefully respond that, yes, I understood that from the beginning, but I didn't know she was a nymphomaniac as well. Still, I'd do it all again, in a heartbeat.

Prologue

I never wanted to be a lawyer. I enjoyed the outdoors as a kid and couldn't imagine being cooped up in a stuffy courtroom day after day. I thought maybe life as a forest ranger was something I'd enjoy.

The thought of standing up and speaking before an audience frightened me. I think I earned a C or C minus in speech class in junior high school. For me, public speaking was hands down the worst thing about school at the time. Curiously, I welcomed singing solos in church and performed a humorous monologue in junior high that was a big hit with my classmates.

I did some acting and had several good parts in high school plays and musicals, along with some gigs as a vocal and instrumental soloist. I sang with a popular folk group patterned after The Kingston Trio throughout high school. These diversions gave me much pleasure and some experience before audiences. So, looking back, I loved the musical performance part of having an audience in front of me, but loathed the speaking part. I'm not sure when that changed, or why. I never spoke in front of an audience in high school or college. Perhaps it was being forced to speak in front of juries that changed my mindset from fear to fortitude. I recall no epiphany or mental effort to make myself more comfortable in public speaking. I just know that I did it.

Sometime during my high school years my classmates and I took the Kudor Preference test. It required students to punch pinholes through a scoring sheet to rank our interests in particular lines of work. My score sheet showed that I was suited for employment as a forest ranger, farmer, or musician. The profession of law wasn't even on the radar.

College didn't jell any ambition for a career, either. Whenever I went back to Cedar Rapids for a rare visit, Dad could be depended upon to ask, "What are your plans after graduation, Johnny?"

Dad majored in journalism but never worked as a journalist, preferring a career in real estate. Part of that grew from the fact that he graduated from college in 1934, in the depths of the Great Depression. He was offered exactly one newspaper job upon graduation, at $40 per week, in Mississippi, 900 miles from home.

A compact and powerful man, Dad stormed Iwo Jima in the first wave of Marines on February 19, 1945, turning thirty-three years old two days later. Wounded after three weeks of fighting, he got patched up, rose from his cot, walked out, and rejoined his unit, fighting for several more weeks until he was wounded severely. My mother received the news of his first wounding the day I was born, March 17, 1945.

Dad was a drill instructor for most of the war, graduating many classes of recruits and draftees before being sent overseas. A strict disciplinarian, he didn't spare the rod, in the form of his right hand. He taught me boxing in a time-tested effort to toughen me up. Once I hit him too hard when we were sparring, after being warned not to. He set me up with a left jab and decked me with a massive right cross that I can still feel in my mind.

During those infrequent visits home from college, Dad and I would walk the dog around the neighborhood. By the time we reached the intersection of Linden Terrace and Crescent Street, about two blocks from home, I could expect The Question.

I was a history major. I had no plan. The Vietnam War was in full swing. I was looking at the draft over my shoulder. I didn't know what I'd do, and told him so, time after time. Despite his Marine's pride, he fully supported my fervent wish not to enter the military in that war.

Then, when The Question came yet again, sometime during the summer of 1966 I was ready. I still had no idea what to do, but wanted to put some kind of end to this ceaseless concern. I told him perhaps I'd try for law school. Somewhat to my surprise, Dad was delighted. There were no lawyers in the family, but he was clearly pleased.

I went back for my senior year more than a bit worried. I imagined Dad proudly telling his friends that Johnny was going to be a lawyer.

By default I started thinking about it. Grad school still exempted students from the draft. Marriage did also, but that wasn't in the picture.

Law schools accepted any major. The only criteria were a reasonably good grade point average and a good score on the Law School Admissions Test. My political science professor was encouraging. He reminded me that a baccalaureate history degree would qualify me for exactly nothing. Not even forest ranger.

So it was that I enrolled in the University Of Iowa College of Law in the fall of 1967. I had a vague idea that corporate law would be a safe choice for me, but I drifted through two years without moving in that direction. Almost half my classmates dropped out, flunked out or, when draft rules changed, were gobbled up by Selective Service. Classes weren't boring, by any means, but nothing grabbed me. Oh, and I got married.

My new wife and I were both students and worked at regular and odd jobs for my remaining time in law school and hers as an undergraduate. I clerked at a local law firm for part of that time and learned much about an operating general practice partnership. I also saw how mismanagement and loose practices can create some major disasters for the lawyers and their clients alike.

In the second semester of my third and final year, I took a trial advocacy course from an adjunct professor. The course's time slot fit my class schedule, and I was coasting toward graduation.

Trial Advocacy was taught by Bill Tucker (his real name), an honest-to-goodness, practicing, successful trial lawyer in Iowa City. I was smitten. Tucker was charismatic, with a deep, authoritative voice and a self-assured bearing. He breathed life into trial work as no other professor could.

After all, the faculty was composed of gifted academics, unskilled in trial practice, but outstanding legal scholars. How could they be expected to generate enthusiasm for trial work when none, to my knowledge, had ever darkened a courtroom door? Occasionally, a professor would sniff at "practitioners," implying some sort of hierarchy by consensus in which law professors were intellectually, if not morally, superior beings.

Tucker got right to work. We studied and practiced jury selection, opening statements and closing arguments, direct and cross examination, qualifying and introducing exhibits, and preparing proofs of evidence. This hard-headed lawyer defined better than any of my more scholarly professors what an advocate is.

An advocate arranges, articulates, interprets, and emphasizes facts in the best possible light on behalf of his client in a way that the client would do for himself if he were trained to do it. With conscientious and effective advocacy on both sides of a contest (and it must be *both* sides) the truth is more likely to emerge than under any other means of conflict resolution.

The pejorative term, "mouthpiece" actually describes well what a lawyer does, standing on his two feet before a judge or jury. And that's exactly what the system encourages and trains lawyers to do. By testing contested facts with sworn testimony, physical evidence and vigorous advocacy, the truth will likely take the form of a just verdict. Exceptions abound, of course, which are often the comparatively few outcomes that make the newspapers.

Tucker also emphasized the practical side of trial work and the details of law practice in a way that rang true because he lived it every day. During that semester Tucker and his partner represented a young man charged in a highly publicized car-pedestrian death case in which the driver hit and ran. I went to the Johnson County courthouse to watch some of the proceedings.

Tucker could do no wrong. In complete control of the courtroom, his opponent, and not incidentally, the facts, he was like a rock star in my eyes. I was hooked. The law came alive for me in that courtroom. I knew what I wanted to do.

I
Baptism

The lady doth protest too much, methinks.
-Shakespeare, Hamlet, Act III, Scene ii

Muscatine, Iowa spreads itself along high bluffs and tumbles down to the west bank of the Mississippi River. Mark Twain lived there briefly and described the sunsets as the most beautiful he'd ever seen. Twain's bouquet to the town is still memorialized on the municipal stationery and on welcome signs along the approaching highways.

Sand deposits left by ancient meanderings of the river are everywhere. Flooded sand quarries are now swimming holes and fishing spots. The sandy soil drains so well that tomato fields break the monotony of corn and soybeans so typical of Iowa farms, so much so that H.J. Heinz maintained a ketchup plant there for decades. Even wild cactus blooms so prolifically that the sons and daughters of migrant tomato pickers who have made Muscatine their permanent home harvest it for a delicacy made from the tender shoots.

As a newly minted lawyer in 1970, I was hired by a father and son partnership in Davenport, Iowa. My salary was $7,500 per year.

Arthur (Jack) Middleton Jr. offered me employment as an associate in the firm. The main attraction was Arthur Middleton, Sr., a crusty, hard drinking, pipe-smoking trial lawyer. I consulted my Trial Advocacy professor, Bill Tucker, in deciding what to do. He said Mr. Middleton was well regarded by the trial bar and had much to offer by way of teaching and as an example. His son didn't enjoy the same reputation as the father but was ethical and hard working.

Tucker told me Mr. Middleton could serve as an excellent mentor and was widely respected among his peers. Tucker described him as a bulldog, which I took to be a good thing. However, he didn't mention the drinking problem. In fairness, he may not have known. I accepted the offer and looked forward to graduation.

Active duty in the National Guard intervened between graduation and the beginning of my career. Toward the end of my training as a field medic I received a cryptic letter from Arthur, Jr. advising that Mr. Middleton had suffered something called a myocardial infarction. His heart muscle was severely damaged. He'd be bedbound indefinitely and unable to work. The news hit me like a thunderbolt.

I was discharged from active duty on November 13, 1970. I bought a 1954 Buick with my final paycheck and drove alone to Iowa from Texas, not knowing what to expect, but anxious to confront whatever awaited me.

Life isn't always fair, but it's life. My first day at the office staggered me. Walking in that first day with a shoeshine and a new white shirt, I accepted the welcomes and good wishes of the staff and Arthur, Jr. with a sense of triumph greater than I felt on graduation day. When I saw my desk piled high with lawsuit files, I fell to earth. Just short of panicked, I took up an avalanche of Mr. Middleton, Sr.'s cases while he embarked on a long recovery.

In the army I learned how to triage patients. Triage is the hard-hearted but necessary practice of treating the most seriously wounded soldiers first, after determining they had a chance to live. In sorting Mr. Middleton's stacks of files needing my attention I performed a sort of legal triage. I reasoned that the thickest files were probably the ones closest to trial, and began with those.

Muscatine County owned the local cemetery, administered through intergovernmental agreement by the City of Muscatine. One of our best clients insured the city. Savarro vs. City of Muscatine, et al was one of my inherited cases, and was comparatively close to trial.

Evelyn Thompson had delivered three babies in quick succession as a young woman, all of whom died in infancy. Being indigent, she couldn't afford to bury them. A kindly family friend had an extra gravesite in the Muscatine Cemetery and offered to inter the first baby in the family plot. Miss Thompson quickly agreed. As successive babies were born, lived a short while and died, they were buried in the same grave on top of each other.

After almost thirty years, the old gentleman who offered the cemetery plot passed away. When his grave was dug for burial, the adjacent grave containing the bodies of the babies collapsed into the opening, bursting open the tiny white coffins and spilling the contents into the new hole. There was nothing for the gravedigger to do but to gather the remains, bring them out of the excavation, and pile them on the fresh dirt and sand.

Miss Thompson, who was by then Mrs. Savarro, was called by the sexton of the cemetery and told of the accident. She hurried to the scene and was traumatized by what she saw. Tiny bones, coffin wood, and baby clothing mingled with the sand, dirt, and other debris of the gravesite.

Evelyn Savarro sued almost immediately. She named as defendants the old gentleman's estate, the cemetery sexton, the funeral home, the gravedigger, Muscatine County and the City of Muscatine. The city turned the suit over to its insurance company, which retained our firm. As a result, I became intimately familiar with yellow sugar sand.

Yellow sugar sand is rounded, large-grained sand that doesn't compact well. Deposits of the sand underlay the Muscatine Cemetery in its lowest area, making grave digging a dicey matter. The investigation showed that a deep vein of the sand at the donor's gravesite had caused the grave holding the babies to collapse into the newly opened adjacent grave.

My job was to work up the "discovery" in the suit to prepare the case for trial when Mr. Middleton was well enough to defend the city in court. I was thrilled to be so directly involved in real litigation. Some of my classmates who wanted to try cases were spending their time in the law libraries of their larger firms, never seeing a courtroom or tasting the exciting work trial lawyers do. Many were becoming bored and disillusioned after working so hard and paying so much to get through school.

One reason I joined the little Middleton firm was that I thought I'd get into the courtroom faster. The sooner a lawyer anxious to handle trial work can get real experience, the better litigator he'll become. Still, I knew I wasn't ready for prime time, all by myself. Even my outsized ego wasn't prepared for solo work.

By far, the discovery process is the greatest part of a lawsuit. It has nothing to do with Columbus or Galileo. It's what goes on before the case reaches the courtroom. The trial is just the tip of the iceberg. As I drew out my discovery plan I thought of myself as a chair-bound battle strategist, laying out imaginary campaigns as I gathered and digested facts and the law that applied to those facts.

Sworn answers to written questions called "interrogatories" help both sides assess what the issues are and what they are not. Properly employed, interrogatories, depositions, requests for production of documents, requests for admission, motions for adjudication of law points, and a host of other procedural means enable the parties to discover the entire picture of the dispute. Once the picture is complete, the lawyers must pare it down to the contested issues of law and fact, like cropping a photograph, for an orderly presentation to the jury. Non-lawyers often wonder why lawsuits seem to drag on for so long. The main reason is the discovery process.

A second reason is that trial lawyers often juggle a great many cases at once, and all demand a share of the lawyer's time. A third reason is that cases must get in line for a court date in a system with a limited number of judges, courtrooms, bailiffs, and staff.

Delay for delay's sake isn't something I encountered often. The real challenge was scheduling matters for depositions or trial with multiple busy lawyers involved. I had a few cases that lasted longer than World War II. Most trial lawyers can say the same thing.

The most valuable and dramatic discovery device is the deposition. A deposition is a question and answer session, on the record, with a court reporter present who takes down every word. The witness is under oath. The lawyers usually agree that rules of evidence and objections are waived, reserved for trial, or limited to allow the parties a broad range of discovery.

The reporter records the questions and answers in a symbol language resembling hieroglyphics mixed with what look like random alphabet letters, and converts these symbols into words. The proceedings are typed and certified by the reporter as a true and correct transcription.

The deposition transcript helps the parties prepare for trial and ties the witness down to a set of facts, which, in most instances, should be exactly the testimony introduced from the witness stand. Material contradictions between trial testimony and deposition testimony present a fertile field for cross-examination. Depositions are admissible as evidence when the witness giving the deposition is out of reach by subpoena, too ill to testify, or deceased.

Depositions allow the lawyers an invaluable opportunity to assess the demeanor and appearance of the witness and to try to predict how the witness will behave before the jury. The lawyers may pose as many questions as they please until the subject matter is exhausted. No judge is present for depositions, and the lawyers enforce their own standards of mutual courtesy and deference. My first unsupervised deposition experience was to depose Mr. and Mrs. Savarro.

Evelyn Savarro entered the courthouse conference room on the arm of her husband, as if she needed help just meeting her responsibility to give her deposition. A tall, severe woman with sharp features, she appeared heavily burdened by the litigation process. Her body language suggested impatience overlain with an unhappy disposition.

The deposition of Emilio Savarro wasn't memorable. His value as a witness was limited to his observation of the trauma his wife suffered after visiting the gravesite, the sleepless nights, the crying episodes, and the loss of enjoyment of life. The usual stuff, I was later to learn. Mrs. Savarro was the main attraction. While her husband testified she sniffed and blew her nose at intervals. Her eyes darted about the room when she wanted to see the reaction among the lawyers to her husband's testimony.

Mrs. Savarro's deposition was consistent with her husband's, with frequent recesses to regain control of herself. Clutching her purse with one hand and her handkerchief with the other, she answered questions in long paragraphs whenever the opportunity arose.

Because I was inexperienced in taking depositions, the lawyers for the other defendants examined Mrs. Savarro first. This made sense, because by the time the questioning got to me, the subject matter would be fully explored and I couldn't make too many mistakes.

To look like I knew what I was doing, I took notes as fast as I could. As I listened to the experienced lawyers and tried to think of an original line of questioning, I began to worry. Nothing came to mind that wasn't already asked. My carefully prepared outline dissolved as my colleagues asked all the questions I'd thought were so original during my preparation. Mrs. Savarro described her loss in such great detail, amid much sighing and tears, that I began to wonder if our client would challenge my bill if I didn't ask anything.

My turn finally came. Some of the lawyers were gathering their papers and closing their briefcases. I had only one question on my list:

JDS: Mrs. Savarro, what were your babies' names?

Silence.

JDS: Mrs. Savarro, would you like the reporter to read the question back?

More silence.

All tears and whimpering stopped. Clutching her handkerchief, she whispered to her lawyer, then, much whispering to her husband. A short recess was taken. When we resumed, her lawyer announced, "For the record, Mrs. Savarro does not remember the names of her babies."

I said, "Mrs. Savarro, has your lawyer accurately stated your testimony?"

She replied, coldly, "Yes."

The deposition was over. The other lawyers congratulated me on my question and seemed especially pleased at the answer. While I felt I had rounded out the discovery picture to some small extent, I didn't realize the power this little exchange had for the entire trial.

A movie director couldn't have provided a more fitting climax to the case. Closing arguments took place a few months later in an August thunderstorm, with much rain and lightning. Wind whistled through the windows of the old courthouse. With so many lawyers involved, I was not asked to participate.

Arthur Middleton, now temporarily recovered from his coronary, centered his closing argument around the woman whose agony over her loss seemed so great, but she couldn't remember the name of even one of her infants. Was her grief genuine or was it motivated by money? The jury decided the case had no merit and sent the Savarro's home with nothing.

Muscatine and our insurance client were pleased. My baptism in the real world of civil litigation put a smile on my face. I knew I was headed in the right direction.

———————

Imagine you're drowning. You inhale a throatful of water, cough, and reflexively try to inhale. Instead, more water comes in. Your voice doesn't work. Worse coughing exhausts the remaining air in your lungs. You silently slip beneath the surface. Your lungs cry for relief. You struggle and flail about, quickly sapping your blood of oxygen as you fight to rise toward the light instead of falling slowly to the bottom, weighed down by water in your lungs where air should be. You realize the awful fact of what's happening, and that you're powerless to stop it. Fright and wild panic overcome you. Accumulated carbon dioxide in your blood triggers a final, paroxysmal gasp for air, only to be met with more water pouring into your lungs.

No one can see you. You're deep in a lake where the water is murky, cold and dark. You're alone in silence, and will soon die. No lifeguard, friend or nameless swimmer will save you because you're invisible.

Your summer outing with friends, so carefree just moments ago, is over just as your existence on earth is over. Water, your life-giving friend and partner in fun, is now ending your life. A dreamy, sleep-like state overcomes you. Imagine you're seventeen years old.

Lyle Shays grew up on a small acreage in the tiny river village of Port Byron, Illinois. The only child of Chet and Martha Shays, Lyle was a big, blond, football player with a blanket of freckles across his nose. Lyle's high school grades were average at best, but with a cheery personality and boundless energy, he was popular among his classmates. One hot Saturday afternoon Lyle and some buddies drove over the bridge to Iowa to swim in an oxbow lake near the Mississippi. The lake was owned by a private firm called Performance Recreation. Performance invited the public to swim there for a fee. Lyle's mother and father engaged Arthur Middleton to represent them in an action against the company for the loss of their son.

Shortly after Mr. and Mrs. Shays retained our firm, and while I was on active duty, Mr. Middleton suffered his heart attack. The file languished until I arrived. I was immediately put to work juggling many more urgent matters, and the Shays suit was among the thinnest folders in my stacks of inherited files.

When I finally looked at the case after a few weeks I was taken aback at being responsible for such a serious assignment at the beginning of both my life as a lawyer and the firm's representation. Mr. Middleton had filed a lawsuit and served it on Performance Recreation. Performance filed a general denial. It was now my job to investigate the dispute, work up a theory of the case, and begin discovery.

Unlike the Savarro suit, I had no other firms of attorneys on my side to lean on in preparation. While by now I had a sliver of experience in handling matters on behalf of defendants, I'd been given no plaintiff's assignments up to then. Mr. Middleton's son, Arthur, Jr., offered some welcome advice on "paper discovery" and sequencing of events that corresponded with what I'd learned in my trial advocacy course in law school, but nothing specific. I decided to take a look at the lake to see what I might learn firsthand.

I filed a Motion to Enter Upon Real Estate for Inspection Purposes, which was quickly granted. It was early autumn. The lake had just closed for the season. A sour and unpleasant insurance lawyer for Performance accompanied me. He wouldn't answer my questions or allow measurements or photos. He correctly noted I hadn't asked for court permission to take any pictures or perform measurements. My first big mistake.

What safety equipment was available when Lyle drowned? I walked around the lake and noticed two lifeguard platforms, one beside deep water near the diving boards and one on a sandy beach with shallow water below some picnic tables. A line of buoys marked the wading area.

I saw no poles that could be used to reach out toward struggling swimmers, nor any life preservers. Instead of the blue or green hues one might expect, the water was a muddy brown. An old rowboat was on shore, turned over.

I worked up what I hoped was a commonsense theory of the case: a municipal swimming pool full of clear, fresh water wouldn't command as high a level of care in providing lifesaving personnel and equipment as a pond or lake, for the obvious reason that victims could be seen under water. In the lake, a lifeguard would have only seconds to see a struggling swimmer and react to what he saw before the swimmer slipped beneath the surface.

No one missed Lyle for over half an hour after he was last seen. The autopsy showed he had indeed drowned. He didn't suffer a heart attack or other immobilizing injury, but the medical examiner couldn't pinpoint the time of death. No alcohol or other drugs were present.

The oval-shaped lake was several times larger than a typical municipal swimming pool. An investigating officer's report showed there were three lifeguards on duty when Lyle drowned. Two were in elevated chairs and one roamed around the lake.

Three lifeguards seemed too few to me, considering the size of the area they had to manage plus identify trouble early due to the opaque water quality. I looked forward to deposing the manager of the facility, who was also one of the owners. Meanwhile, I needed to find out more about Lyle.

It stands to reason that a lawyer almost never knows the victim of "wrongful death," as it's called, before death occurs. So it behooves the lawyer to get acquainted as much as possible with the deceased before trial, not only to be able to introduce a stranger to the jury, but to develop the measure of loss as well.

I learned that Lyle wasn't a dedicated student and probably not bound for college. He wasn't a star on the football field either, but his coach described Lyle as among the hardest working players he'd ever coached. Photos provided by the family showed a happy, smiling kid enjoying what turned out to be the best years of his life.

Lyle painted houses and barns in the summer of his death and worked part time stocking shelves at the village grocery store. He'd never earned over $1,000 a year in his short life. Why is this important? Courts recognize the intrinsic value of life can't be measured in money. Besides compensation for pain and suffering, Iowa and Illinois law provide that judges and juries are allowed only to determine the net loss to the deceased's estate if he would have lived to a normal age. The deceased's habits of thrift, earnings, spending habits, and savings all contribute to a picture of what such an estate might look like.

If the deceased is married, the surviving spouse and children also have claims for loss of support, services, and companionship. Because the Shays were Illinois residents, Iowa would apply Illinois' law of wrongful death damages to the accident occurring in Iowa.

In 1971 the measure of death damages for an unmarried minor, with no career, no firm prospects for one, and an insubstantial record of earnings to present to a jury was next to worthless. Courts would refuse to entertain evidence of future earnings and savings on the grounds that the proof was deemed too speculative. Pain and suffering damages, though excruciating and awful to contemplate, were in reality quite brief.

I deposed the dour manager of Performance Recreation. He'd been prepared well: ramrod straight, hands folded on the conference table, good eye contact, and direct answers to my questions.

The initial gleanings from his deposition were individually rather small potatoes, but together they painted a picture of a profit-driven enterprise with little thought given to safety. For one thing, there was no limit to the number of patrons the company would admit at any one time. Only two seated lifeguards and one roving guard were felt sufficient to protect perhaps two hundred patrons in a large water surface, with all levels of swimming ability.

For another, no periodic breaks were taken. It's common at municipal pools to call swimmers out of the water hourly for ten-minute periods both to rest tired swimmers and allow lifeguards to scan the bottom. Here, because the water was unclear, Performance felt there was no need for breaks. Finally, there were zero life preservers on hand.

What *was* available? The answer stunned me. Patrons could rent giant tractor tire inner tubes to float around on. The manager testified under oath that the inner tubes were suitable for rescue. How far could they be thrown? Maybe fifteen feet. Were ropes connected to any of the tubes so a swimmer lucky enough to reach a thrown tube and hang on could be pulled to safety? Well, no. Were any such ropes even available? No again. Were any tubes kept close to lifeguard stations so they would be handy in an emergency? No, he said, the tubes were kept in the concession area where they could be rented by patrons. And anyway, he offered, the tubes didn't matter because Mr. Shays wasn't seen by anyone before he sank beneath the surface. At this point I sorely wanted to argue with the witness. *Of course, sir, and why do you think we're here?*

I didn't hold my tongue because I was well disciplined and professional. I wasn't. I kept quiet because I was too inexperienced and timid to speak out. But I was more disgusted than angry.

The manager also pointed out the old rowboat, which I'd noticed at my visit. He thought the boat might be useful as a rescue device, even though it wasn't near the deep water lifeguard station.

Anything else? The lifeguards were certified and changed position every ninety minutes. That was it.

The manager acknowledged that once a swimmer went underwater without being seen, his rescue was almost impossible. He testified helpfully that there'd been no drownings at the lake in the twenty or so years of its existence.

I felt management had just been lucky. However, even a perfect safety record is almost never admissible as evidence. For example, say a trucker runs a red light and kills a pedestrian in an intersection. Evidence that he stopped at ten thousand red lights in his career before the accident is irrelevant.

In our case Performance practiced a lethal combination of inattention and disregard. And that attitude took the life of Lyle Shays.

I often spent spare moments thinking about Lyle, and my heavy and unaccustomed responsibility in representing his estate and his parents. Had I thought of everything? Was I too biased, seeing only the trees, or was I able to see the forest as well? I decided to ask my secretary what she thought. After all, she knew the file almost as well as I. She'd been typing letters, briefs, court motions, and internal memoranda since the day the case began.

The following morning I called her into my office and asked her to imagine she was on the Shays jury. If she felt persuaded that Performance Recreation was not at fault, what would she say to convince her fellow jurors of her view? She took a deep breath, thought for a moment, looked me in the eye and said softly, "Accidents will happen."

Of course! How obvious! Those three words jolted me like a bucket of ice water. It brought me down to reality, making me face a deeply sobering question: how could I have missed this? And how could I begin to counter such a self-evident defense?

I started losing sleep. I was forced to consider that if Mr. Middleton wasn't recovered I'd have to try the case myself. I could ask for a postponement, but I stood the chance of being unable to persuade the judge that Mr. Middleton might not be able to return to trial work in the near future, or ever. No, I had to prepare for trial against experienced and competent insurance lawyers representing Performance Recreation as though I'd be Chet and Martha's only chance. I couldn't assume that Mr. Middleton would be there to take command.

I glanced in the mirror one day and decided I looked too young. I grew a mustache to try to look older. It itched. It was reddish. Janelle, my wife, hated it. My secretary hated it. I told them they'd get used to it. They did. Or, at least, they stopped complaining about it.

I reminded myself that Chet and Martha Shays had engaged Mr. Middleton, not me. While they surely knew I was inexperienced and liable to make mistakes at trial, was their unspoken confidence in me well placed? Should I have a heart-to-heart conversation with them about the prospect that Mr. Middleton might not be available for trial?

I decided against it, and resolved to do everything I could to address an "accidents will happen" mindset with my only weapon: the evidence. I drew out a flow diagram on yellow sheets of legal size paper. I placed each fact supporting all elements of Performance's fault in a column on the far left. Next, I compiled a correspond-ing column with the names and testimony summaries of all witness who could support each claim. The next column contained what I assumed would be counter arguments and witnesses Performance would call. My final column contained my rebuttal to Performance's strong points.

While a rudimentary analysis at best, and one that would change many times before trial, the diagram helped me pull together the strengths and weaknesses of the dispute. Perhaps just as impor-tant, it gave me some measure of confidence that I was in control of the facts, as my mentor, Bill Tucker, always was.

Although my detailed breakdown of the evidence in Lyle's case gave me some temporary comfort, I slowly began to understand that worry is the constant companion of the trial lawyer. Mowing the lawn, paddling our canoe on a pleasant afternoon on the river, and even the hated National Guard summer camp failed to banish the crushing worries of the moment from my head. I tried to worry about only the problems I could deal with, and separate from my mind those over which I had no control. I resolved to deal with Mr. Middleton's possi-ble absence from the trial when and if it happened, but not until then.

As the case moved forward, Arthur Middleton slowly improved. He'd tried Savarro vs. City of Muscatine successfully, but the trial sapped his strength and landed him back in bed. He took time off to recuperate before the Shays trial, and toward the end of 1971 was well enough to attend and participate. Wan, weak, and much thinner, he seemed to perk up as I briefed him about the case. As I'd hoped, he said I would serve as "second chair" and handle a major part of our presentation.

I was elated. I'd been responsible for shepherding Lyle's case to trial, my first big jury case, and I knew it backward and forward. I'd tried to ask myself the hard questions and provide answers to prob-lems of proof, logic, strategy and argument. I'd been waiting for this chance to work with Mr. Middleton and learn at his feet since joining the firm over a year before.

The trial finally began on a sunny Monday morning. As our first witness, I called the now-nervous manager who had to defend the giant tractor inner tubes as rescue devices. Nervous myself, but hoping not to show it, I was able to win several points. Asked what the rowboat was good for, after a victim slipped below the surface, he testified, "The lifeguard could row out and look for bubbles."

Out of the corner of my eye, I caught a juror shaking her head slightly. During a short break as the manager left the witness stand, Mr. Middleton whispered, "Not bad." I could have kissed him.

After four and a half days in the courtroom, Arthur Middleton was hitting home runs like Mickey Mantle, time after time. He was on a mission, and it showed in his voice, his energy, and his color. His "lunch break" was a bowl of Capstan pipe tobacco on the courthouse fire escape, alone in thought.

The jury's body language seemed to favor our side, with the arms of several jurors crossed during defendant's presentations and bodies leaning forward during ours. Expecting a whipping, the lawyers for Performance approached us suggesting serious settlement discussions.

I'd lived with Lyle's case for over a year, and his parents and I had become close. Being personally invested in the case and now quite sure in my inexperienced mind of a huge verdict, I urged Mr. Middleton to decline all proposals. He took some time to think about the final offer and consulted with Chet and Martha. Late that afternoon, without telling me, he accepted $30,000 in full settlement.

I was unhappy, both because he settled, and with the amount of the recovery. Looking back, $30,000 seems a pittance. However, the amount was well within the boundaries of wrongful death settlements for minors in 1971, and Chet and Martha were happy the ordeal was over.

It's hard to believe, in the second decade of the twenty-first century that $30,000 could ever have been a fair amount to compensate the family for Lyle's wrongful death. But it was. If Lyle had lived he'd be fifty-eight years old now. Since his death, and too late for Chet and Martha, the rules of evidence have been much relaxed, allowing for a statistically-based picture of a deceased minor's potential as an earner and saver. The changes are for the better.

And, it's always possible we would have lost. But I didn't think so then, and I don't think so now.

II
Vengeance

Hell hath no fury like a woman scorned.
-William Congreve, The Mourning Bride

Dating back to the early 1900's, lawyers concentrating in the defense of insurance lawsuits often got their start as claims adjusters. When I began my career in late 1970, there were few firms left that also investigated and adjusted, or settled, insurance claims. Our little firm was one of them. The only client still requiring our adjusting services was Ludke Brothers Motor Freight, a small regional self-insured trucking company.

I was the only lawyer in the office one drizzly February morning in 1971 when I took a call from the home office of Ludke Brothers. The caller first asked for Arthur Middleton, Sr. Mr. Middleton was still recovering from his heart attack. He then asked for Arthur, Jr., who was away. Would the caller like to speak to Mr. Stonebraker? He would.

A few minutes before, a semi-trailer truck had pulled out from a warehouse driveway into the path of a Ludke Brothers truck at a curve on River Drive, a main thoroughfare entering Davenport from the south. The impact was severe. I was to grab my camera and tape recorder and get to the scene, fast.

I wasted no time. When I arrived I saw that the Ludke Brothers truck was a "cab-over" box truck model, with the huge windshield just in front of the driver, who sat over the motor. A wrecker had just pulled the truck back from the point of impact–square in the middle of the semi's trailer. Seatbelts in trucks were rare then. I watched as Ludke's unbelted driver was removed from the shattered windshield and transported to the hospital.

I asked the crowd if anyone had seen the accident. No one had. I took some pictures and measurements, went back to the office, and made my report.

When he was well enough, I went to the hospital to interview Ludke's driver, Ralph Couranian. Ralph lived near Davenport in a neighborhood populated with families of Armenian descent, as he was. Ralph was married and had been driving for Ludke Brothers for several years.

Ralph was a mass of bandages and casts, having two broken legs, one hip, and several ribs. One lung had collapsed. He suffered severe lacerations on his face and upper body. For a time it was thought Ralph might not pull through. His jet black hair and two black eyes were all I could see of his features.

Ralph and I were different, but we got along well. He had a good sense of humor in spite of his terrible pain and knew he was lucky to be alive. On one or two occasions he was either asleep or too groggy from his medications to talk. I had his authority to look at his chart, and marveled at the stoicism of this badly broken man.

Our town had attracted Armenians for two or three generations. In the previous century, an immigrant might find work at a local industry like John Deere, prosper, and get word back home that the area was a good place to live and work. Whole families and portions of entire towns and villages would emigrate to this promised land. Armenians tend to marry other Armenians. Many traditions, values, customs, and superstitions still survive from the old country. Fortune telling is common. Old hurts are never erased. Grudges are passed down from one generation to the next. A Turkish army massacred over 200,000 defenseless Armenians in 1896, and the far-distant tragedy is still remembered yearly among Armenian-Americans in Davenport, Iowa. Honor, disgrace, humiliation, and retribution are values that run deep among this proud people.

Years later, when I was at the courthouse on other business, I saw a group of Armenian-Americans surrounding a person in a large hallway outside a courtroom. They were chanting rhythmically in their language and pointing in unison at a woman in the center of the circle. I learned that the woman was testifying against another Armenian. The group evidently thought this was a betrayal of the community. Such was the culture among this closed, almost insular group.

I visited Ralph several times. His recovery was slow. Another operation was required after several early surgeries performed just after admission. I became acquainted with Linda, his wife, and her mother, an Armenian immigrant.

After weeks in the hospital, Ralph developed pain in the groin area, a high fever, and great discomfort on urination. Tests were ordered. On top of all his other difficulties, Ralph was diagnosed with a raging case of gonorrhea.

How could this happen? Only one way, Sherlock. Ralph and Linda managed to have sex in his hospital bed somehow, in spite of his almost paralyzed condition. Obviously, Linda had been busy during Ralph's lengthy hospital stay.

Ralph confronted Linda angrily, and a shouting match erupted. Previous indiscretions and infidelities were trotted out and aired on both sides. Heads poked out of doorways, and orderlies were called to calm things down. Linda went home in a fury, packed her things, and, for good measure, set fire to their house.

I couldn't represent Ralph in his claim against the trucking company causing the wreck because, in representing his employer and worker's compensation carrier, my firm had a conflict of interest. Ralph made a poor choice of lawyers and received only a small settlement for his nearly mortal injuries.

The Ludke Brothers truck had a tachygraph, an early device that recorded the truck's speed constantly on a rotating paper wheel that corresponded with the time. The lawyer for the semi's insurance company was able to show that while Ralph was driving within the speed limit at all times before the wreck, he may have been traveling too fast for the wet conditions, a defense based on reasonableness and due care. The wet surface of the road coupled with the curve leading to the accident scene was dangerous, he argued.

Under Iowa law at that time, Ralph's possible negligence, (or fault) provided the semi's insurance company with a complete defense to its own bad conduct. Ralph's lawyer couldn't overcome this hurdle and settled for a small amount rather than taking a chance on losing in court.

In later years, most states have seen the unfairness of applying a strict standard of "contributory" negligence as a complete bar to recovery and have adopted a fairer standard known as "comparative" negligence. In this way, the jury is allowed to compare the fault of each party to the total fault causing the accident and award damages based on the percentage that the injured party's fault bears to the whole. If comparative negligence had been the legal standard at the time, Ralph's case would have been worth substantially more because his share of fault causing the accident would have been comparatively small.

Ralph's homeowners insurance company didn't honor his claim for the destruction of his house. His policy, as do most policies, provided that even an innocent spouse is barred from recovering when the other spouse is guilty of arson. Ralph was left with his meager worker's compensation benefits, a small injury settlement, permanent and disfiguring injuries, no wife, and no house.

Marital retribution isn't uncommon. A few years after the Ludke Brothers wreck, an auto insurance company we represented got a call from an insured's ex-wife. Still burned by some marital injustice, she told them to search a flooded sand quarry in Muscatine County. She said we'd find her former husband's car there, sleeping with the fishes. He'd reported it stolen some years before, when a repair estimate was more than he wanted to pay. Our insurance company paid the claim when the car didn't turn up.

We decided it was worth the effort to try to find the car. Water in sand quarries tends to be relatively clear, and professional divers were available. But which quarry? The ex-wife didn't know. Muscatine County is pockmarked with sand quarries. We talked to the County Engineer, who knew every mile of the county by heart. In an effort to narrow our search, we assumed that the quarry holding the car would probably be near a road. The driver would want to step out at slow speed after putting the transmission in gear and letting the car find deep water near shore. The County Engineer identified several quarries fitting our assumptions, narrowing the scope of the investigation considerably.

We employed a diver and began our search. Sure enough, the third or fourth quarry we checked produced our "quarry," as it were. The car was found just off a gravel road in forty feet of water, below a small rocky cliff.

Our satisfaction in finding the car was tempered by the challenges of retrieving the evidence needed to convict the owner. It would have cost too much to retrieve the car from the murky deep. Renting a large construction crane and transporting it to and from the quarry was far too expensive. Fortunately, our diver had an underwater spotlight and camera. Photos of the license plate, still affixed, the vehicle identification number and his ex's testimony were enough to charge and convict the startled owner. He pleaded guilty to insurance fraud and filing a false police report.

———

Our firm grew over the years, and one of my partners handled divorces for a period of time. She had great rapport with her largely female clientele, and built a fine reputation as a "go-to" lawyer for domestic disputes in our community.

One of her clients had been around the matrimonial block a few times and enjoyed a torrid relationship with a young man for about a week. They were deeply in love and spent a romantic summer night nestled in a blanket in a meadow under the stars, entwined in each other's arms. As they watched the sunrise, he tenderly gave her a symbol of his undying love. On his knees, he asked her to marry him. Overjoyed, she accepted. The symbol was a pinecone.

Life was idyllic for a time, but things went south. The undying love died. She consulted my partner, and after an unsuccessful effort at reconciliation, divorce papers were filed.

Practitioners of matrimonial law are generally despised and reviled, often justly. Lawyers can easily aggravate an already bad situation by deliberately egging on the spouses toward a goal of seeking vengeance rather than justice. Of course, the attorney's fees rise proportionately. In most cases, however, the lawyer hates the discord, the anguish, and the human cost of divorce work day after day and year after year, and sees little personal satisfaction from his efforts. In this case, as often happens, the roles were reversed. The parties themselves pitted the lawyers against each other for their selfish satisfaction. The couple had no children and few personal effects, but what little they had became the subject of unending dispute.

The centerpiece of the contest was the pinecone. Both parties wanted it. They wanted it so badly they would sacrifice anything to hurt the other. "The pine cone lady," as she became known around the office, called during the day, night, and on weekends. Nothing could dissuade her from checking on her case and unburdening herself on the subject of her husband. If her lawyer wasn't in the office, she was only too happy to declaim to the secretaries on her problems or even call her lawyer at home.

Iowa law provides for a 90-day waiting period before a divorce decree may be entered, at the earliest. This battle went on for well over a year, with little to show for the time and money spent. She paid her bills by borrowing from friends and family.

My partner patiently explained several times that the pinecone wasn't worth the huge investment in an effort to have it awarded to her, but to no avail. At lunch one day we decided among ourselves that we'd gladly offer her a new pinecone, gilded in gold if necessary, just to be able to get the case settled and close the file. One partner had a better idea. "Hell, just give it to the wife and give the husband pine cone visitation rights!"

A lawyer can't "fire" a client in litigation without good cause, and even then, court approval must be obtained. Violation of this rule gives rise to a claim for a species of malpractice called "abandonment." My partner felt she was a prisoner bound to this unfortunate woman, but couldn't seek court approval to withdraw her representation because she had no grounds.

The case eventually went to court. I don't recall who was awarded the pinecone. I have no doubt, though, that our client is still complaining loudly to whomever will listen that she spent thousands in divorce fees for nothing.

She's right.

III
Fraud

The difference between stupidity and genius is that genius has a limit.
-Attributed to Albert Einstein

The courthouse is viewed as a chance to win the lottery by some. The odds at the outset, at least, are fifty-fifty. On paper, you might win, or you might lose. A certain share of plaintiffs and their lawyers alike hold this view. When times are hard, more and more suspicious cases appear on the docket, and juries can sometimes be fooled. When a city bus is involved in an accident in large cities like Chicago, it's not unknown for pedestrians to jump *onto* the bus to be in a position to present a claim for injuries. I was never involved in anything that blatant, but enjoyed defending fraudulent cases as much as any I dealt with.

Insurance fraud is rampant in good economies and bad, but becomes more common when people are out of work and desperate. Since it's impossible for every false claim to be discovered, it's just as impossible to determine how much economic damage undiscovered fraud does to both the insurance industry and society, owing to unjustified verdicts and settlements and the enhanced "risk premium" fraud adds to every policy.

For a time I worked with a small team of investigators from several companies whose job was to bring insurance fraud cases to ground. Some were easy and some not. Some slipped through the cracks and couldn't be solved. A few even turned out not to be fraudulent after all.

One case involved a neighborhood restaurant owner who couldn't sell his business. To improve his profits, he hired two small-time crooks who shoplifted meat from supermarkets and sold it to him for his menu. The crooks would make the rounds of several supermarkets daily, buy a few groceries or cigarettes, pay for them, and slip the meat past the checkout counter in their bulky overcoats. This went on for over a year. When no buyer for his restaurant appeared, the owner adopted Plan B. He hired his shoplifting team to burn down the restaurant so he could collect the insurance. The crooks would share in the booty once the check came through.

Late one summer night after closing, the perpetrators jimmied the lock leading to the restaurant basement to make it look like breaking and entering. The owner was a controversial citizen and no doubt had many enemies. He wanted the fire to look intentional because neither he nor his co-conspirators knew enough about arson to make the fire look accidental. He was careful to have an alibi in the form of a poker party with many witnesses who could vouch for his whereabouts.

The miscreants lugged a big can of gasoline down the basement stairs and spread the gas around on the floor. The plan was to light a match as they went back up the stairs and made their escape. But they hadn't counted on the pilot light on the gas water heater.

Before they reached the stairs, the gasoline fumes ignited with a loud WHOOOMP, blowing out a basement window and arousing the attention of a woman living in an apartment across the street. She soon saw two men running to their pickup truck, their clothing ablaze. Amid much cursing and shouting the truck took off, trailing smoke. The police were called, who, in turn, called the unsurprised owner, who called his insurance agent.

The agent was well acquainted with his insured and his financial problems, put two and two together, and called a member of the fraud team I was associated with. The team member did a simple thing. She alerted all the major hospitals she could think of within 100 miles that any burn victims presenting themselves for treatment should be reported to the local police.

The arsonists were soon arrested at the Burlington Community Hospital, ninety miles away. They quickly confessed that they'd been hired by the restaurant owner, and the investigation was closed. The firebugs and the owner pleaded guilty to arson, and the insurance claim was denied.

The charred restaurant was soon bulldozed and became a successful barbecue spot, one of my favorites. Smoke again rises from the site, but now it's sweet-smelling hickory smoke from a popular eatery.

———————

Florida is a fertile source of wholesale used cars for two reasons. First, retirees are still moving to Florida in large numbers. Elderly people drive their cars less and less as they age, but many can't bring themselves to sell them. Their Mercedes's, Buicks, Fords, and Volvos may sit for years in their garages, with no mileage being added, until the owner's death brings them to auction.

Second, Florida cars don't rust. No salt is put on Florida roads in winter. Low mileage Florida automobiles purchased cheaply at estate auctions with flawless bodies bring high prices in Midwest markets.

There's a thriving business in buying, transporting, and selling Florida auction and estate vehicles in the upper Midwest. Smaller dealers pay a driver to individually bring a car north for resale, but the larger rust belt dealers invest in car transports to fetch eight or more cars at once.

One large dealer decided to defraud his insurance company. He reported a full load of high-end used vehicles stolen with his transport while he left it running at a truck stop in Tennessee. He claimed that after dinner and a shower, offered to truckers gratis, he returned to where he parked the transport to continue his trip to Iowa. The transport and its valuable cargo were gone. Authorities in several states quickly sent out stop orders and searched the highways and byways, but not a trace of the transport nor any of its autos could be found.

The call's origin at a Tennessee truck stop checked out, but inconsistencies in the dealer's story led his insurer to suspect something. An exhaustive investigation over several months found nothing. Neither the transport nor any of the cars it carried turned up, in spite of a nationwide computerized alert network. Strange.

Then our fraud team discovered the owner had a minor criminal record that wasn't disclosed on his application for an Iowa dealer's license. This nugget triggered greater scrutiny of the claim.

The team decided to rent an airplane and flew over a remote piece of Florida land owned by the dealer's brother. There, hidden under palm trees and tropical foliage, was the empty car transport. Another flight with a powerful camera gave us all the evidence we needed. The insurance company denied the claim, on the general grounds that the dealer had given a false statement on his claim form. He promptly sued.

I took the dealer's deposition. At first, he was cooperative, affable, even friendly. Soon, however, he gave me the opportunity to experience one of the few and highly coveted, "Perry Mason Moments" in a lawyer's career.

After about an hour of questions, I asked about the transport. What was its make, model, cab color, capacity and year of manufacture?

He told me.

JDS: Do you have any pictures of your transport?

WITNESS: No.

JDS: Would you like to see some?

Stunned silence. Court reporters are trained to keep a stone face, but I thought I heard a gasp from her direction. I marked several photos as exhibits to the deposition. The confident, friendly witness was now noticeably uncomfortable.

JDS: Take a look at Exhibit A. Is this your truck?

WITNESS: Looks like it.

JDS: How about this one?

WITNESS: Same answer.

JDS: How about this one?

WITNESS: Where'd you find it?

JDS: The rules allow me to ask questions, not answer them. Is this your truck?

WITNESS: Looks like it.

JDS: Would you be surprised if I told you your truck is on your brother's property in Florida?

WITNESS: I don't know.

JDS: Do you have any idea why your truck would be located on your brother's property?

WITNESS: Nope.

JDS: Do you know how it got there?

WITNESS: No.

JDS: It never made it up to Tennessee, did it?

WITNESS: Sure it did. I drove it.

JDS: Do you have any idea why your truck would be hidden from view?

WITNESS: I can't say it looks hidden.

JDS: Do you know how far your truck is from any road?

WITNESS: No.

JDS: Do you know why it's sitting in this underbrush?

WITNESS: No.

JDS: You don't see any car or truck dealerships around in this aerial photo, do you?

WITNESS: No.

JDS: No evidence of civilization at all, is there?

WITNESS: No.

JDS: Nobody would have reason to make a delivery of a BMW out there in the jungle, would they?

WITNESS: I don't know.

JDS: You don't have any idea why your transport is down there on your brother's property, empty?

WITNESS: No.

JDS: Big surprise to you?

WITNESS: Very big.

The dealer's only real surprise was the appearance of our photos. He and his lawyer dismissed the claim. The automobiles were never found.

Perhaps because the fraud involved three states and many jurisdictional issues, the dealer was not prosecuted. But a satisfying victory came when his dealer's license was revoked. I came to learn that much white collar crime goes unpunished. There are several possible reasons, but the most likely one is that criminals charged with white collar crimes can afford better lawyers. More about that later.

One type of fraud is almost impossible to prove. The "set up" is a street intersection the perpetrator has identified beforehand. It's usually a city street intersecting with another street carrying fairly heavy traffic. It's controlled by a stop sign, with the sight distance to the left somewhat obscured by hedges, trees, or buildings. Every town has several such places.

Here's how it works. The perpetrator makes sure he has a vehicle behind him as he pulls up to the pre-selected intersection. He stops, looks right and left, then appears to pull out into the cross street. While he's doing that, the driver behind looks left, assuming the first car is safely continuing through the intersection. He begins to drive forward past the stop sign.

Suddenly, the first driver stops and a low impact rear end collision ensues. It then becomes a contest of fact between the drivers, the "injured" party claiming another car had come from the obscured area to the left, and the second driver claiming not. Juries tend to believe the first driver's version because he's out in front, with the better view.

Considerable sums have passed from insurance companies to "injured" drivers under this scenario. Fortunately, there's now a national database of sudden emergence claims. A driver may get away with one such claim, but he's unlikely to get away with a second.

Most lawyers and the public at large believe garden variety rear-end collisions are automatic winners in court, but they're not. Improvements in medical technology and automotive engineering have indirectly helped defense lawyers defeat many spurious injury claims.

However, low impact collisions can indeed cause real extension-flexion, or "whiplash" injuries. These claims involve "soft tissue" trauma that can't be proved or disproved by traditional X-ray interpretation, CAT scans or other generally accepted means. Rather, they're supported by palpation by the physician, often a chiropractor, who claims to feel telltale stiffening of neck muscles called muscle spasm.

They'll testify that muscle spasm indicates the body's misguided effort to protect itself from a vertebral misalignment, or "subluxation," in the delicate neck structures. Spasms can't be faked, and aren't always present. They're often strangely absent when the victim is attending an independent medical evaluation arranged and paid for by the insurance company defending the hapless rear-ending motorist.

Chiropractors also have developed non-traditional X-ray criteria known as George's Line. If a chiropractor detects that one or more of the spinal vertebrae have strayed from a predetermined curved line drawn from a point on one vertebral body through several more on the X-ray film, he feels justified in confirming the patient's complaints.

Almost every spine, healthy or not, has small anomalies that may confound evaluation based on George's Line, but that doesn't dissuade chiropractors. And, even assuming the validity of the diagnosis, unless a victim has a pre-existing condition making him susceptible to serious injury, such minor trauma usually clear up within around six months following the collision.

Chiropractors are widely accepted in the communities where I practiced. Palmer College of Chiropractic is located in Davenport and used to grandly call itself, "The Fountainhead of Chiropractic." Chiropractic was "discovered" (some say invented) by B.J. Palmer, an eccentric radio pioneer in Davenport who purportedly cured a janitor's deafness by manipulating his spine.

Early claims for chiropractic as a cure-all for almost every human ailment were still common when I did most of my defense work. Chiropractors were usually deposed at their offices as a convenience to them. I used the opportunity to gather as many pamphlets and other literature in the doctor's waiting room as I could. I then cross-examined him on his claims for chiropractic "cures" available for such diverse maladies as liver ailments, asthma, kidney malfunction, high blood pressure, digestive disorders, female problems, and even acne.

Before chiropractic groups successfully lobbied the Iowa legislature to require health insurance carriers to cover their bills, it wasn't uncommon for chiropractors to accumulate thousands of dollars in unpaid bills until a trial or settlement produced a windfall. Where the patient has no health insurance coverage, chiropractors still accumulate substantial bills with little or no payment from the plaintiff, hoping along with the plaintiff for a big settlement or judgment. Obviously, this detracts from their supposed objectivity, making them vulnerable to cross-examination.

If neck complaints lasted much longer than six months after a low impact accident or the treating physician or chiropractor opined that the condition was permanent, I could be pretty sure I was dealing with a fraud case. The miracle of human healing is too powerful for the great majority of previously healthy low impact accident victims not to recover fully, given a little time.

A permanent condition is the mother lode of large jury awards, because under Iowa law, the plaintiff's lawyer can build a *per diem* argument for the jury based on the plaintiff's actuarial life expectancy, bringing a small or non-existent injury into the stratosphere of financial compensation. For example, if the jury decides the "pain and suffering" of the plaintiff is worth only ten dollars per day, a younger plaintiff with thirty years of life ahead of him (10,950 days) may be awarded $109,500, and tax free to boot. Injury verdicts and settlements are not "income" under the IRS definition. Rather, the funds are compensation for an injury and not taxable.

Add to that, testimony supporting a projected loss of earnings (taxable) and loss of enjoyment of life (not taxable, called "hedonic" damages), and verdicts can double. Adding still more verdict potential is the commonly heard expert testimony that traumatic arthritis will be reasonably likely to develop, and is permanent and progressive. Taken together, these elements of damage can add up to hundreds of thousands of dollars in extreme cases.

Courts allow a reduction to the present value of future damages, but some economists will readily testify that the effects of inflation over many years will cancel out present value discounts, making present value arguments moot. Juries are invited to grant a verdict of a dollar today for a dollar's worth of pain experienced since the accident, tomorrow, next month, next year and for every future day in the injured person's life. Juries may be attracted to this invitation because no math is required to calculate "time value".

The concept of present value vs. time value is easily understood. For example, buying a $25 government bond might cost $19.25. Over time, the value of the bond becomes $25, and the bearer cashes it in at maturity. Thus, the "time value" of a $25 bond is $25 seven years after purchase at a "present value" of $19.25. However, inflation may frustrate the profit in the transaction if the purchasing power of $25 today is more than $25 in seven years.

As mentioned, testimony that the alleged injury will be likely to cause arthritis or worsen existing arthritic changes can greatly swell a verdict for the plaintiff. Spousal and children's claims for loss of services, society, companionship, and "consortium" (generally thought of as a fancy word for sexual relations) with the injured spouse can add around ten to twenty percent each to the basic claim.

Part of my strategy in trying rear end cases was to admit fault in causing the accident, and train the spotlight on the unlikely nature of the injuries. As the auto industry gradually improved safety devices, insurance defense lawyers gained advantages in the courtroom.

Improvements like shoulder belts, air bags, collapsing steering wheels, padded dashes, head rests that block the rearward extension of the head and neck, anti-lock brakes, and the advent of collapsing automobile frames designed to dampen impact all made injuries less likely. I noticed over the years that heartbreaking photos of maimed accident victims became a less-frequent occupational hazard.

Energy-absorbing bumpers and frames spare many motorists and passengers from injury and greatly reduce the severity of injuries to others. In low-impact collision cases, juries usually awarded zero damages, but occasionally would award just medical expenses and a tiny bit more.

I found analogies could drive home my causation defense. If the causal link between a minor accident and a claim of injury was weak, an analogy in closing argument could help the jury see my way of thinking. Here's my favorite, a true family story.

Our family has a big white dog called a Great Pyrenees. He weighs 185 pounds and his name is Sherman Tank. Sherman spends the night outside on his leash and also when we aren't home. When he's outside, he thinks he's protecting us. We live about two blocks from the railroad tracks that wind along the Mississippi. It's a fairly busy rail line.

Sherman always hears the trains coming several minutes before we do. He has an enormous bark. He starts barking, and keeps it up until the trains have gone by and he can't hear them any longer.

We had a family conference about this problem. The neighbors don't complain. They're too polite. But unless we were to bring Sherman in the house and keep him inside all the time, his barking promised to be an ongoing embarrassment. We couldn't seem to teach him not to bark at trains. It was part of his instinct.

Our oldest son said, Dad, look at it from Sherman's point of view. He thinks he's doing a great job. Since he's been around, not a single train has dared to come into our yard.

Sherman misunderstands something that confuses humans, too. It's easy to mistake cause and effect. And that's what he does.

I hope you don't make the same mistake Sherman makes. Don't confuse cause and effect. The plaintiff and her lawyer want you to believe her claims of constant pain come from this tiny collision.

My guess is, you know better.

I tried and won enough rearward impact cases that some disappointed plaintiff's lawyers dubbed me "Mr. Rear End." I loved the double meaning.

Although I was properly prohibited from arguing many of these claims were based on fraud, the jury could usually tell. I couldn't mention the possibility of fraud because under the rules of evidence, I couldn't usually prove it and didn't have to. First, the standard for proof of fraud is "clear and convincing evidence." This standard is below the criminal standard of proof called "beyond a reasonable doubt," but substantially higher than the usual civil standard of a mere preponderance of the evidence.

"Preponderance" is defined as "the greater weight" of the evidence, or just enough to tip the scales. The "clear and convincing" standard is more amorphous, but also much more restrictive.

Second, the law doesn't require the defense to prove anything. The burden of proof rests with the party trying to upset the status quo, that is, transferring money from one table in the courtroom to the other.

Some final observations about my experience with chiropractic: in thirty years spent trying injury lawsuits and settling hundreds more, I never saw a single claim of whiplash in company with other objective, demonstrable injuries, such as broken bones, knocked out teeth, a concussion, or lacerations. Claims of minor neck trauma were without exception the only claims made in whiplash lawsuits.

But if chiropractic is not scientific or reliable, what explains the experience of patients who genuinely report improvement? Obviously, I'm not a doctor and have comparatively little medical training. Ten weeks spent learning how to be an army medic is all the training I have, short of studying medical texts and articles and consulting with experts in preparation for trials. I believe there are several explanations.

First, the placebo effect is extremely powerful and, paradoxically, poorly understood. Clinically, we know it exists because of the way science works. Medical studies are most reliably performed with the "double blind" technique. Simply stated, half the ailing subjects in the study receive the medicine or treatment being evaluated, and half receive a sugar pill or non-therapeutic treatment called a placebo, with no known effect.

Neither the scientists administering the study nor the subjects know which patients receive the real medicine or treatment, and which receive the worthless placebo. Only the study's evaluators have the information to correlate administration of the medicine with results, and compare the placebo's effects with the real thing.

Ideally, only the medicine or treatment being evaluated should show positive results in reducing or eliminating the condition. But strangely, some of the subjects receiving the placebo improve as well or even better than patients in the other half of the study who receive the genuine medicine. Almost mystically, not only do some placebo recipients show improvement, but the healing can be confirmed with objective, scientific tests.

How could this happen? Nobody knows. The patient's conscious mind thinks the body has received real medicine, but it hasn't.

Somehow, the subconscious self believes the condition will improve after administration of the artificial medicine or therapy. The body rises to the task and heals itself in remarkable and almost metaphysical ways. In fact, if the physician expresses confidence to the patient that his pills or other treatment will work, a higher correlation of placebos to improvement has been reported.

Of course, cure or improvement by placebo doesn't happen in most cases, but when it does, it qualifies as a true medical miracle. Norman Cousins wrote of the phenomenon in a first person account of his response to a mysterious and debilitating disease, titled, *Anatomy of an Illness.* He recalled a conversation he had with the renowned Dr. Albert Schweizer. Schweizer acknowledged the phenomenon, and said it has been a secret physicians have known since Hippocrates. He called the placebo effect, "the physician who resides within."

Schweizer commonly saw real healing triggered by African witch doctors performing dance rituals and incantations, and administering such treatments as taps on the patient with "magic" sticks and whispering in the patient's ear. Perhaps some favorable chiropractic results can be chalked up to the placebo effect.

Second, as noted before, the God-given curative powers of the body generally repair typical extension-flexion stresses and strains of the neck and back within around six months. Chiropractic treatments may do no harm, and often provide some temporary relief. But their results may closely track the calendar, with durable improvement owing to the passage of time being credited instead to the manipulative treatments.

Third, and I have no direct support for this theory, it seems to me patients who report back or neck strain due to working in the garden or a fall on their own icy driveway tend to recover much faster than patients who are hurt in an accident that's someone else's fault.

The medical community has a term for patients involving the legal system in their condition who don't recover in a reasonable period of time. When some doctors have observed their patients, treated them, tested them and ruled out every reasonable cause of continued complaints, they dub the condition, "compensation neurosis." The community of defense lawyers has another term for it. They call it "the green poultice effect". Money tends to cure a lot of ills.

A case I lost in Cedar Rapids involved a man working at the iconic (for Iowans) Kinnick Stadium, the football venue at the University of Iowa in Iowa City.

The plaintiff, Orville Jensen, was a crane rigger and oiler employed by one of many subcontractors on the general renovation project. I represented the supervising contractor overseeing the subcontractors performing multiple improvement projects around the stadium. Jensen was perched on a brick wall, helping guide a huge new scoreboard into place with the help of a crane. The crane was so big it couldn't be assembled inside the walls of the stadium. The operator was manipulating the crane blind, outside the stadium with the boom over bleachers in the end zone. A spotter at the top of the bleachers gave the operator hand signals.

A gust of wind pushed the suspended scoreboard like a kite on a string, knocking the plaintiff-to-be off his feet. He landed hard on the bleachers, breaking his hip. His fracture healed normally, but X rays showed minor deformation from what doctors call "anatomical" shape. Jensen claimed our client should have stopped work once wind gusts made the crane work dangerous. I defended the general contractor on the grounds that the crane company was in control of that decision and better able to judge the limitations of working in breezy conditions. The crane company felt work shouldn't be stopped, and our client honored that decision. Jenson couldn't sue the crane company because it was his employer. Worker's compensation was his sole remedy against it.

The trial lasted around ten days. Mr. Jensen appeared every day with his wife. He had a pronounced limp, and relied on a beautifully carved cane for support. Testimony was undisputed that he was never without his cane, and I accepted that evidence without challenge. His luxuriant mustache and twinkling eyes conveyed an outwardly friendly and non-confrontational frame of mind, with nothing to hide.

The jury disagreed with our defense and awarded a generous sum of money to the plaintiff and his wife. Our insurance client paid the judgment without appeal.

A few weeks later, the court reporter for the case told me she'd seen the plaintiff in a local store. He was walking normally. Neither his limp nor his cane was anywhere to be seen.

I credit his "recovery," several years after the accident but only weeks after the trial, to "the green poultice" principle. Some litigation-minded citizens are suddenly cured when a lawsuit is over, whether they win or lose.

Physicians themselves are constrained both by their training and the legal system. In their training, they're taught to conclusively presume that the patient's complaints are real and work backwards from those complaints, methodically trying to find out what's wrong.

It's understandably frustrating for a dedicated practitioner of the healing arts when he fails to find an objective cause for the patient's continued discomfort or failure to heal. The physician is reduced to becoming an advocate for his patient, no matter what his personal beliefs. No wonder most physicians hate the courtroom.

Often out of frustration the doctor sometimes refers the patient to a pain clinic where mind exercises, meditation, yoga, acupuncture, nutrition, soft music, and other modalities are tried in a final attempt, often in vain and always expensive, to reduce or eliminate the discomfort. When that fails, the pain clinic's goal is reduced to helping the patient "learn to live with it."

When all reasonable resources are exhausted, the physician is barred in the jurisdictions where I practiced from testifying that in his opinion the patient is malingering, or falsifying his condition. Rather, the physician must resort to finding a label for the problem in an effort to explain the unexplainable.

Occasionally, "compensation neurosis" is the diagnosis. In lay terms, it's all in his head. That is, the hope of being paid money for an accident is causing either an imaginary physical problem or a hypersensitivity to one's health that shows up in physical complaints. The "injured" person sees a window of opportunity to improve his financial wellbeing, if not his physical health.

When a conventional diagnosis is not made and the physician remains unable to isolate a cause for a patient's complaints, the frustrated physician is at a loss. By the lights of the medical profession, a yawning gap exits in the field of diagnostics. The patient has seemingly unrelated complaints but no medical label for his problems. In spite of hundreds of years of advancement in the science of diagnostic medicine, nothing cures the patient and the doctor must admit defeat.

Or must he? Enter a new condition labeled, "fibromyalgia." Literally, fibromyalgia means tissue pain. Physicians have devised a diagnosis for fibromyalgia which includes some eighteen seemingly unrelated locations on the body, called, "trigger points," where the physician places light pressure.

Fibromyalgia trigger points fall into no known neurological pattern. Medical scientists have decided that if eleven (why eleven?) or more these locations produce a report of pain by the patient, fibromyalgia becomes a candidate for the diagnosis.

Fibromyalgia is a "diagnosis of exclusion," meaning when all other possibilities are ruled out, fibromyalgia, relying as it does solely on the patient's report of pain, can become the label for his complaints. Thus, a scientific-sounding moniker is placed in the patient's chart, which the majority of the medical community now recognizes as a valid diagnosis.

Over time, fibromyalgia has become legitimized by consensus. Most physicians have become so fond of fibromyalgia that it has managed to find a place in *The International Classification of Diseases,* the hallowed and usually authoritative compendium of recognized illnesses compiled by the United Nations' World Health Organization and relied upon by the medical community for decades.

While the validity of fibromyalgia and its diagnosis is beyond the scope of this book, it's worth noting that the condition strikes a much higher proportion of women than men, without a medical explanation for the disparity. Some of the proposed causes include such diverse agents as breast implants, accidents, lupus, electromagnetic hypersensitivity, parvovirus, thyroid disease and irritable bowel syndrome. It's also been linked to mental conditions including general stress, menstrual anxiety, memory loss, and depression. In fact, underlying chronic depression is closely correlated with a diagnosis of fibromyalgia. But correlation is not causation. Whether the former gives rise to the latter, or vice versa, or neither, is an open question.

As mentioned, the law bars the physician from offering an opinion that a plaintiff is malingering, or faking an injury or illness. Such opinions call for a statement of "ultimate fact." In other words, truthfulness, or the lack of it, is something that only the jury can conclude, not an expert with years of training and experience in the field.

Lawyers can go up to the edge of a suggestion of malingering, but not over the edge. Defendants' physicians may testify that a patient's complaints have no basis in objective testing. They may also opine that no causal relationship appears between the plaintiff's complaints and the accident that is the subject of the suit.

Plaintiffs' lawyers counter by securing admissions that there's no test that can measure pain, and that the doctor can't say the patient's complaints "aren't real." Sometimes juries are confused by all this, and sometimes not.

Trial lawyer Louis Nizer wrote, "Truth does not fly into the courtroom. It has to be dragged in by its heels."

One of my early trials involved a blind intersection, but the facts were different from the fraudulent rear end "set up" scenario discussed earlier, and the collision was significant. The damages suffered by the plaintiff were partly real and partly not.

Bob Markham pulled up to a stop sign at Locust Street, a main artery in Davenport, from a side street. A high terrace obscured his view of a motorcyclist fast approaching from his left. Bob pulled out. The cycle smashed into the driver's side of his small pick-up. The motorcyclist, John Michael Browning, was thrown over the hood and traveled about fifty feet in the air, breaking both bones in his right forearm.

The police investigator found a loaded pistol on the pavement, which Browning admitted was his. He had no carry permit. I was unable to bring these facts into evidence because the judge ruled (correctly) the issue was irrelevant.

Browning's arm healed slowly and required a metal plate anchored with screws to join the fractures. By the time Browning recovered, his doctor testified the bones were actually stronger than before the accident. This result is not unusual in healthy people because the body often goes overboard and lays down more bone in an effort to heal the fracture than the victim really needs. This news was highly disappointing to Browning, who harbored hopes for a large insurance check.

When settlement negotiations proved unsuccessful, Browning sued. In discovery he claimed he had to give up rugby, with all the unprotected rough and tumble activity that goes with it, because his arm ached constantly. He was afraid it would break again in spite of his doctor's assurances that it was stronger than before it was broken. I accepted his position with some reservations, reasoning that having experienced a serious trauma he could honestly decide he didn't want to invite another.

Browning also claimed the metal plate in his arm absorbed heat from his body, making the arm constantly cold. His doctor said he could easily remove the plate since it had done its work, but Browning refused.

He claimed he couldn't find employment in spite of unrelenting efforts. Browning was suited for manual labor but said he wasn't as strong as before the collision. He was also a little unusual in that he'd earlier brought suit for back injuries against the local Holiday Inn after an unwitnessed fall on ice while delivering clean towels as a laundry delivery man.

Browning claimed permanent back injuries from his icy fall, although he played rugby for years afterward, right up until his accident with Bob Markham. To avoid a lawsuit, the motel's insurer paid an impressively large settlement.

I confirmed almost accidentally that Browning had indeed played rugby at one time, at least. The rear bumper on his car parked in his lawyer's lot bore a sticker reading, "It takes leather balls to play rugby."

At the time I was a medic attached to a helicopter unit in the Iowa Army National Guard. At a weekend drill I happened to mention this case to another lawyer in my unit while the case was pending. Another guardsman, Jim Stafford, overheard me and said he knew Browning well. They were members of the same rugby team. Jim said Browning hadn't quit the squad following his injury as he claimed. In fact, my fellow guardsman was the team historian and kept a scrapbook.

Stafford thought he had a recent team picture with Browning in it. He also remembered that Browning was off the team for a few months after his accident and spent several weeks of that time touring Europe.

I drove straight to my office after drill that Sunday evening and reviewed the interrogatories and other discovery served upon me by Browning's attorney. Still in my green class C uniform and army boots, I carefully examined the file.

There was no question or other discovery device that required me to update any of our responses and provide the damaging information to Browning's lawyer. I decided to call Jim Stafford as a so-called "rebuttal" witness. The sole purpose of a rebuttal witness is to contradict the testimony of another witness on a material and contested fact.

Under the rules of civil procedure there's no duty to disclose the anticipated testimony of a rebuttal witness. In fact, there's no requirement even to place the identity of a rebuttal witness on a list of witnesses supplied to the Court and opposing counsel before trial.

Although "trial by ambush" has almost been eliminated by the rules of discovery, rebuttal remains a vestige of the element of surprise. The wisdom of allowing rebuttal witnesses without a corresponding requirement to disclose the identity and proposed testimony of the witness is to prevent a chance for the contradicted witness to "adjust" his testimony before the rebuttal witness is called.

In my opening statement I admitted fault in causing the accident, and that Browning had sustained a genuine injury. However, I advised the jury that we were vigorously contesting Browning's claim of severe and continuing injuries.

The jury was treated to another rare "Perry Mason moment" when Jim Stafford took the stand and told the jury that Browning was in Europe for weeks when he claimed he was job hunting. He testified Browning played rugby on the team just as before, and didn't appear to hold back or play less aggressively following his accident. We introduced several post-accident photos, both action shots and a team picture, all with Browning prominently identified, as rebuttal evidence.

The defense closing argument almost wrote itself. The plain contradictions in Browning's sworn testimony and the words of Jim Stafford's independent testimony set up the argument for a link to a common experience some of the male members of the jury encountered every day. Here's an excerpt:

"Ladies and gentlemen, you heard an unbiased rugby club teammate, Jim Stafford, tell you Mr. Browning was playing rugby while claiming to you under oath that he gave it up for good after he broke his arm. You have the rugby team pictures before you. Those pictures can't speak out loud, but they tell quite a story, don't they? Mr. Browning played rugby the entire season after his arm healed and the season after that. Right up until the present day, in fact. But he told you he quit. He wants you to order us to pay him for having to quit rugby when he didn't.

What else? He told you he looked every day for a job after the doctor released him. But it turns out he was discovering the pleasures of the great capitals of Europe for almost a month while claiming he was beating down doors looking for work.

Mr. Browning had a chance, under our rules, to contradict Jim Stafford, or even call him a liar. He produced no contradicting testimony at all, from himself or anyone else. He could've told you Jim was biased, or had a grudge, or was simply mistaken. But remember what his lawyer said when Judge Dupre' asked him if he had any witnesses after Jim left the stand? "No, your Honor," is what he said.

When my son was a little boy, he'd put his hands over his eyes and think I couldn't see him. Mr. Browning and his lawyer are doing the same thing. They have their hands over their eyes, hoping you can't see the falsehoods in their case, and their total failure to answer the proof of them.

Now let's take a second to look at the metal band on my wristwatch. In the wintertime, when men put on their metal band wristwatches in the morning they're momentarily cold but soon warm up to body temperature. They don't draw heat away from the wrist all day long, making the wrist feel cold. You gentlemen know this from your personal experience in life. In fact, the metal on wristwatches and bands has a much larger surface area than the plate in Browning's arm. You can see that from looking at the plate shown in his X-rays in your evidence file.

Why does this matter? It matters in two ways. First, Mr. Browning's "cold arm" complaint makes no sense when you look at our experiences in daily life. Second, Mr. Browning refused a low risk procedure to remove the plate in his arm. It had done its work, stabilizing the fracture of two bones while his arm healed.

Nature did its work, too. Browning's doctor also told you his forearm bones were even stronger than before the accident. His doctor told you the plate could be removed quite easily if Browning wanted it done. But he didn't.

He could have the "cold arm" problem fixed for less than fifteen hundred dollars, the doctor said. But his lawyer just stood up and told you with a straight face that he wants twenty-one thousand dollars to compensate Mr. Browning over his lifetime for his cold arm alone.

It seems likely to me, at least, that he would rather complain to a civil jury about his supposedly cold arm than make himself better. He's clearly lied to you, not once, but multiple times, to inflate his claim.

What's the bottom line in all this? Just this. You can't penalize Mr. Browning for lying to you. You should deal with Mr. Browning fairly, but firmly. Enter an award that reflects his real injuries, not what he says they are.

Browning received a small verdict from the jury, proportionate to his legitimate injuries. The verdict was a victory, considering what his lawyer had demanded in settlement, and far less than what we'd offered before suit was filed.

I might have lost Bob Markham's case but for that chance conversation at my weekend national guard drill. But, as the saying goes, luck is the residue of hard work.

———

Occasionally marital disharmony joins with fraud in creating unusual fact patterns. Late in my career I was assigned the defense of a straightforward rear end collision case involving a husband and wife. Asking over two hundred thousand dollars in damages, Jennifer Tilden sued her husband, Ivor. Her injuries included a serious concussion, a broken nose, minor facial cuts, and a couple of missing teeth. I concluded the injuries were genuine, and Ivor, my client, caused them.

While spouse vs. spouse lawsuits are unusual, they aren't unheard of. The reason is insurance. If an insurance company denies a claim for damages when a husband and wife have a collision, the injured spouse can't sue the auto insurance company directly in Iowa. She must sue the spouse, triggering the obligation of the insurance company to defend him.

The Complaint pleaded that Ivor, in his pickup truck, followed Jennifer's car toward their garage. Ivor braked, but his foot slipped off the brake onto the accelerator. His truck lurched forward into Jennifer's car, causing her injuries.

The accident happened in Waterloo, Iowa, some 160 miles from Davenport. I had a recorded statement from Jennifer, taken by the insurance investigator. Her statement confirmed the facts alleged in the Complaint. As was my usual practice in rear end cases I admitted negligence and began discovery based on an approach to evaluating the claim for money damages.

I decided to meet Ivor on my next trip to Waterloo to talk further about the case and assess how he might appear before a jury. We met at a fast food restaurant. Ivor was a red haired, blue-eyed, athletic appearing young man. He enjoyed riding his enormous motorcycle parked outside, which he proudly pointed out to me.

I was impressed with Ivor's personality and felt he would present well before a jury. Having no reason to doubt the underlying facts, I asked some basic questions about the accident and the aftermath. Innocently, but with a certain relish, he proceeded to tell me a far different story from the one his wife had told the insurance investigator, and as claimed in the suit.

For some weeks before the accident Ivor had suspected his wife of seeing another man. He felt he knew the identity of the man and from time to time checked at the man's house across town to see if Jennifer's car was there. On the day of the accident he drove his truck over for a look-see and was just about to reach the other man's house when his wife drove by in the opposite direction.

Ivor knew Jennifer had no reason to be in that remote end of Waterloo unless she was up to no good. He saw her and she saw him. She hit the accelerator and took off. The street was too narrow to make a U-turn on the spot. Blind with anger, Ivor sped a quarter mile the other way until he came to an intersection, turned around, and tore after Jennifer.

They reached their house at almost the same time, with Jennifer in the lead. She opened the garage door with her opener and almost got inside. Ivor gunned the engine and rammed the back of her car as hard as he could, propelling it into the rear wall of the garage and pushing the front end part way through the wooden structure. The impact tore the overhead frame apart, and the garage door fell flat on his hood.

Divorce proceedings and a civil suit followed as night follows day. Obviously, the accident was no accident. It was an intentional act.

This knowledge placed me in the worst ethical dilemma I ever faced. Jennifer's attorney may or may not have known the truth. She may have told him the crash was unintentional. I didn't know Jennifer's lawyer, and make no claim he participated in a fraud. In any event, he pleaded a set of facts consistent with Jennifer's tape-recorded story that Ivor's foot slipped off the accelerator. Until the moment of my conversation with Ivor, neither the investigator, nor the insurance company, nor I had any inkling that the facts were different from the Complaint filed in Black Hawk County District Court.

An intentional act causing injury voids coverage in automobile liability insurance policies. If I advised the company, which paid my bills, that its insured was guilty of an intentional act, Ivor wouldn't have insurance to cover any judgment against him.

On the other hand, the Iowa Supreme Court has invoked what is called a "tripartite relationship" among the attorney, the insured, and the insurance company. The rules require that the duty of an attorney retained and paid by the insurance company is exclusively to the insured, not his insurance company. I would be breaching the attorney-client privilege if I disclosed the truth to the company, and violating my exclusive duty to the insured as well.

The rules of ethics were making me a party to a fraud. And there was no way out.

I went back to the office, not knowing what to do. I felt I could tell no one without breaching the attorney-client privilege. I made certain no notes or other memoranda were placed in the file to betray the confidence between Ivor and me.

After consulting published comments and explanations of the relevant rules of ethics, I decided I could confide in my partners. We held a meeting to discuss the situation. All agreed I could do nothing to alert the company.

I spent several anguished weeks in limbo. I couldn't justify spending my time and the company's money pursuing discovery, knowing the facts as I did. On the other hand, I had a clear duty to vigorously defend Ivor Tilden. But worse, I couldn't ask him to lie under oath and say his foot slipped. Then I'd be a party to perjury. True, I'd admitted fault in my answer to the Complaint some months earlier, but Ivor's deposition under oath was sure to be part of the discovery. My only course was to contest Jennifer's claim for damages as best I could. But how could I stand by silently and watch the insurance company pay a fraudulent claim?

I was utterly unable to decide what to do. Therefore, I did nothing. I made general references to the press of other business in my reports to the company in an effort to cover up my lack of progress.

Then one day I received the surprise of my life. In my mail that morning was a document from opposing counsel dismissing the case. I called Ivor immediately and asked what happened. It seems Ivor and Jennifer got back together and dismissed the divorce complaint and the lawsuit, too. All was love and kisses again. I was saved.

I don't know how I would have handled matters if the case had continued. Sometimes rules get in the way of common sense. Fortunately the insurance company I represented understood the situation I was in, and forgave me.

I've since wondered if I should have presented the situation to the state bar association's ethics committee for an advisory ruling after the dust settled. Perhaps an exception to the strict "tripartite" rule of exclusive representation should be considered.

I used this dilemma as a case study in a seminar topic I presented at a state convention of defense counsel and asked for suggestions on how I could have proceeded. None of the attendees had any.

IV
Expertise

An expert witness is anyone from more than 100 miles away who carries a briefcase.
    -Lawyers' maxim

Some trials are won or lost not so much by the competing lawyers, but by their competing experts. With few exceptions, experts are the only witnesses allowed to offer opinions to the jury. Consequently, some individuals make a handsome living as experts and consultants to lawyers, who gladly pay for opinions that assist their clients. Lawyers call them "professional witnesses."

When I began practicing, I had an unhealthy reverence for experts, both for my side and against it. I reasoned that they knew more than I did, after all. After trying cases for a few years, I developed almost the opposite opinion.

I opposed a certain engineering expert many times who qualified in hundreds of cases in a wide variety of disciplines. I once heard him testify that fire resistant insulation wasn't really fire resistant because, after applying a flame with a gas torch, it glowed red when he blew on it. It stopped glowing when he stopped blowing, but that didn't matter. He also claimed there was no substantial difference between the terms, "fire resistant" and "fire proof" although federal standards say otherwise.

I heard another hired expert testify that a private swimming pool was unreasonably dangerous because an uninvited, drunken young party goer who became quadriplegic was entitled to a label warning him not to dive into shallow water from the base of a child's water slide. The list is almost endless.

A surprising side benefit of becoming a trial lawyer is the self-education that necessarily flows from preparing for trial. Neurology, orthopedics, metallurgy, fluid dynamics, heat transfer, meteorology, vehicular accident reconstruction, hydrology, economics, fire cause and origin, optics, pesticide composition, paint chemistry, psychology, frozen food preparation, and hospital construction are among subjects I became familiar enough with in narrow areas to be comfortable examining and cross examining expert witnesses.

Of course, a little knowledge can be dangerous. I found myself knowing a little bit about a lot of things. I sometimes worked with consultants engaged to help me understand technical matters. In P.G.(pre-Google)times I could usually scratch the surface of a subject and find enough to work with, and be done with it. But occasionally I had to dig deeper and soon got in over my head. As one consultant put it, in a pitch-perfect impression of the old Saturday Night Live Gilda Radner character, "One thing leads to anothah."

I was often impressed with experts and learned much from them. Late in my career I was part of a group of lawyers representing several defendants in a complex "sick building" case. We engaged a team of highly qualified physicians from George Washington University to evaluate six women who claimed they suffered immune system collapse as a result of working in a poorly ventilated office building. The team's strict methodology in examining the plaintiffs, evaluating the claims, and providing direction and testimony on behalf of the defense team gave us a strong platform for both cross and direct examination.

Similarly, I defended a dairy company in the waning days of home milk delivery. An outside wheel of a rear dual wheel assembly on a milk truck broke away from the hub, rolled down the road, and crashed through an oncoming car's windshield, killing the driver.

Microscopic metallurgical analysis performed by our expert showed telltale fatigue fractures in the lugs on the hub. An unmistakable pattern of fractures showed the failure resulted from sequential tightening of the lug nuts around the circumference of the wheel, like a clock face. Instead, the industry requires alternate torqueing across the wheel diameter. Sequential tightening bedded the wheel to the hub unevenly, causing the wheel to wobble.

As the dual wheels rolled down the road, the rotation slowly bent the lugs back and forth like a wire coat hanger, eventually causing them to fail. Our expert put the finger of blame on an independent tire company employed by the dairy, absolving the dairy from liability.

Although I usually handled defense cases, I would sometimes accept a case on the Plaintiff's side that appeared to have merit. A lawyer from Clinton County asked me to evaluate a situation in which a single woman named Janet Koleg had skidded off a curve to her death on a snowy highway. He felt poor road maintenance might have played a role in causing the accident.

Janet worked as a dishwasher in a Clinton restaurant to support herself and her mildly retarded son, Andrew. To stay off welfare and make ends meet, Janet had an early morning newspaper route in a farming area south of Clinton.

As a kid, I sometimes delivered papers on my bike for a friend who was ill or out of town. The worst routes were those with long driveways or where the houses were far apart. Short routes where customer's houses were near one another increased profits, and less time was required to complete the route. I learned this lesson again a few years later as one of the last door-to-door Fuller Brush salesmen.

Delivering newspapers to farm mailboxes a quarter mile apart showed tremendous character in this otherwise ordinary woman who would not accept charity or welfare. She was delivering papers at 4:30 am on a windy, cold winter night when she died.

I wanted to help. But how? My first reaction was to decline. The woman died in a one-car accident in a snowstorm. Who else could be to blame? My conservative nature and what I knew of the facts told me there was no case, but I promised to investigate and decide later.

I obtained the state accident report and found the highway at the scene was snow packed and drifted when Janet lost control. I went out to look at the location and found I was familiar with it. It was on the same back road I often took to the Clinton County Courthouse, and I'd noticed bad winter driving conditions there on several occasions.

I checked state accident frequency records and found that, although traffic counts were fairly low, the accident rate at this location was slightly higher than average. I then correlated the dates of the accidents to the monthly NOAA weather reports for the previous ten years and concluded most of the accidents where Janet died were winter storm-related.

I decided to have one of my partners interview a farmer who lived nearby. The farmer said there were many accidents at the curve, especially when snow had fallen, because drifts accumulated at the curve in the roadway. The state's Department of Transportation had never placed snow fencing there.

Then the game changer: many accidents went unreported because (before cell phones) uninjured drivers would trudge to the farmhouse, call a wrecker to pull them out, and be on their way. The farmer would place lanterns and flares at the site until a wrecker arrived. Winter accidents were so frequent there that he kept a stock of lanterns and flares on hand earmarked for this purpose.

If there were injuries or if other help was needed, the farmer would call the Clinton County Sheriff's office. The county would send a patrol car and perhaps and an ambulance. These were the accidents that showed up in the state statistics. Of course, the unreported accidents did not. This meant that the true accident experience at this location was much higher than state statistics showed.

I felt we might have a case, but we needed help. The state of Iowa may not have had enough advance knowledge of the danger at this location, but I felt they *should* have known and taken steps to reduce or eliminate the drifting.

I needed someone to help me understand the criteria, if there were any, for placement of snow fencing. I consulted every expert source I knew and turned up nothing. My partner, never one to give up, somehow discovered an authority on, yes, snow drifting. A meteorologist in Washington State had developed a special interest in snow behavior and had written several articles on the subject. He was contacted and agreed only to examine our case. He did not agree to write a report or testify on our behalf. His reluctance was a good sign. I was leery of experts who unconditionally agree to take a case before doing any work. They tend to develop opinions favorable to their clients whether or not they can be supported by the facts. An expert who remains noncommittal until he knows all the facts is likely to be objective and more credible.

He flew to Iowa, examined the scene, took elevation and linear measurements, studied the accident records and weather data, and developed the opinion that the Iowa Department of Transportation had failed to meet minimum standards for placement of snow fencing at the accident location.

He pointed out a small rise in a field to the west of the roadway and said it acted much like an airplane wing, or airfoil. A moving airplane wing speeds the air passing over the curved surface on top. Lower pressure above the wing's surface provides lift. Similarly, a low hill can speed the flow of air passing over it, only to slow it down after it passes. As the air slows, snowflakes fall to the ground, causing drifts.

Sand dunes behave much the same way as the hill at the site of Janet's death. In fact, an entire dune creeps in the direction of prevailing winds over time. Kill Devil Hill, on the Outer Banks of North Carolina, has moved several hundred feet from where it was when the Wright Brothers flew the first airplane there in 1903.

To draw out the analogy further, icing on airplane wings doesn't cause a crash because the airplane becomes too heavy. Rather, the crash occurs because the ice disturbs the flow of air over the wings, destroying their ability to provide lift.

I learned that drifts accumulate on the downwind, or leeward side of a hill due to these characteristics of airflow. Snow fencing on the leeward side, or even on the hill itself, interrupts the airfoil causing drifting to take place before the snow arrives at the highway. Slats in the fence slow and diffuse the wind carrying the snowflakes. The flakes drop to earth, creating drifts in the field on the downwind side of the snow fence, sparing the highway.

Due to the usual west-to-east wind patterns on the Iowa plains, north-south roads are more at risk for drifting. Iowa roads tend to follow the four points of the compass in rural areas, owing to the layout of farms originally surveyed in the 1830's. This highway ran generally north and south, and turned southeast at the curve in Janet's direction of travel. Our expert felt strongly that the accident location would require installation of snow fencing if the Iowa Department of Transportation had exercised ordinary care.

So far, so good. We filed suit against the State of Iowa and proceeded to investigate the state and county maintenance standards and records for this location.

County records showed that a county road maintainer had cleared the west lane of the two-lane highway about two hours before the accident. The highway had drifted shut again in response to high winds and rapidly falling snow, according to Janet's accident report and NOAA hourly wind and precipitation records. Although north-south roads tend to drift much faster and deeper than east-west roads due to prevailing winds, we found the state's maintenance criteria were the same for roads in all directions.

After a few depositions I thought we had enough to win. The Attorney General's office felt so, too. A settlement large enough to provide a generous lifetime annuity for the support of Andrew Koleg was placed with a highly rated life insurance company.

On subsequent winter trips to Clinton I noticed snow fencing placed where it should have been all along. Then the state completely re-engineered the road at the site of Janet's death by increasing the curve radius and slope, and grading away the hill causing the drifting.

I felt we did more than obtain justice. We had perhaps indirectly saved lives and avoided some serious injury accidents by calling attention to an unappreciated danger.

V
Creativity

I will find a way or make one.
-Hannibal

Iowa is a "good government" state. It is, by habit, virtually free of scandal and corruption. Iowa has blessedly little history of voting irregularities, pay-offs, pork projects, and untoward special interest influence. However, I found myself suing the state for a Pennsylvania company that had good reason to complain.

Simpson Saws was a specialty maker of huge circular cutting blades favored by governments and private contractors engaged in highway construction. Tipped with industrial diamonds and bathed in cooling water, the blades cut through concrete like warm butter. Iowa, like all northern states, develops frost heaves in the spring when the ground thaws. Even strong concrete roads can buckle above the powerful effects of the expansion and contraction of the alternately freezing and thawing subsurface.

Road reconstruction requires a substantially larger portion of state budgets in northern states. The buckled concrete and iron rod is cut out, the subsurface re-compacted, new rod placed and tied, and concrete re-poured. This expensive process takes place over the summer months and begins all over again the following spring.

Simpson Saws had provided saw blades worth several hundred thousand dollars to the state for a season of road reconstruction, but hadn't been paid. Simpson added carrying charges and sent several bills without a response. No one claimed the blades weren't delivered and used. No one claimed the blades were defective or didn't perform as expected. The Department of Transportation just didn't pay.

The company was mystified. Simpson engaged our office to get the attention of the deadbeat, in this case the Iowa bureaucracy.

I wrote one or two letters to the appropriate office in the Department of Transportation and, like Simpson, received no response. My client, disgusted, directed me to sue. I sued. What appeared to be a straightforward suit on an open account taxed my patience and prompted some creativity in trying to secure redress for the ignored and highly displeased Pennsylvania client.

"Are we going to have to take time away from business to come out to Iowa and go to court?" the exasperated CEO demanded.

"So it would appear," said I.

"What's the matter with your state?" he shouted through the phone.

I had no answer.

Uncharacteristically, the Iowa Attorney General's Office didn't enter an appearance, motion, or responsive pleading in the suit by the deadline provided by law. As Arthur Middleton used to say, I don't mind being insulted, but I hate to be ignored.

I filed a motion for default against the State of Iowa and received an order entering the default. This procedure conclusively presumes fault in failing to pay a genuine debt and provides for a hearing on the amount of damages due. I supplied documentation and an affidavit sufficient for the court to enter judgment in the full amount of the claim, plus interest and court costs.

Now what? I had to collect on the judgment. I reviewed the statutes and found little to go on. For nearly two hundred years, the doctrine of sovereign immunity protected states from suit. This principle was handed down from the English system of laws and is founded on the idea that the king can't be sued because by definition and divine right, he can't be wrong.

Sovereign immunity ended when states realized that litigation and the threat of it causes states to be more responsible to the public. Citizens injured by government wrongdoing should be compensated just as though some private entity caused the damage. The principle applies to most kinds of wrongdoing, including unpaid accounts.

But I was finding it hard to nail down legal means for collecting judgments against the state. I could file a lien against the local state highway commission storage building, but a judicial sale wouldn't come close to satisfying our judgment. Perhaps partly for my own enjoyment, I wanted some better, more dramatic way of getting the state's attention.

I decided to file a judgment lien on Interstate 80. Conveniently, this major highway passes through Scott County, Iowa, where I lived and worked. Simpson's CEO liked the idea. He was finally gaining confidence that something would happen and his firm would be made whole.

Foreclosure on judgment liens is rare when the debtor has the means to pay, because the threat of losing one's property usually causes the debtor to pay up. I had no plan to foreclose. I just wanted to see if I could rouse some bureaucrat in the state capitol of Des Moines to realize the jeopardy the state was in.

My ploy didn't work. The state filed no response to my lien on the busy highway. My follow-up letters and calls went unanswered.

I hated calling Simpson's CEO to report my chronic failure to get the state's attention. My threat of a lien foreclosure on Interstate 80 seemed so promising in theory but it had failed in practice, like so many of my ideas. I couldn't blame him for being angry. It was the simplest of cases, yet nothing I tried put the money on Simpson's books. It was as though the state bureaucracy and I were living in parallel universes. My judgment award was significant, and I hadn't recovered a dime.

Now what? I felt like the dog that finally catches the bus and doesn't know what to do with it. Could I garnish Iowa's bank account? That sounded complicated, and the bank was in Des Moines, three hours away. Could I put a gate across the highway and collect tolls until the judgment was paid? A fun idea, and the CEO liked it, but certainly not. Could I put the highway up for sale to satisfy the judgment? Again, highly doubtful.

I stepped back, trying to think outside the legal box where I felt most comfortable. There was only one thing left that I could think of to do. I contacted our local state representative in the legislature and sent him my documentation. I included a copy of my lien on Interstate 80. I asked him to cut through the bureaucracy. Aghast, he did. My elected representative was prompt and effective. And, of course, he helped us for free.

An Iowa State Treasury draft arrived within days for the full amount of the judgment, prejudgment interest, post judgment interest and court costs. The fear and embarrassment of possible nationwide publicity in foreclosing a lien on Interstate 80 finally had the desired effect.

———————

Bill McKee was an old friend who operated a small insurance adjusting firm for many years before retiring to Texas with Agnes, his wife of almost fifty years. A jovial pipe smoker with glasses so thick his eyes looked as big as quarters, Bill was always ready with a quip or a little advice, based on his long experience in the insurance industry.

The McKee family home rested comfortably in a bucolic setting of almost twenty acres, with a pleasant creek running through it and huge oaks scattered about. Over the years, the city grew up around the property, which became quite valuable.

Bill and Agnes had no business experience to speak of but they had a great idea. Before retiring they formed a family corporation they dubbed "Pearls, Inc." "Pearls" comprised the first letter of the names of each of their six children.

With legal help from another firm specializing in real estate Bill and Agnes subdivided their homestead into twenty-one spacious lots and borrowed several hundred thousand dollars from a local bank to improve it with streets, sewer, water, underground electricity, and phone wiring. A first mortgage on the property secured the loan.

Since Pearls had no credit history, Bill and Agnes were required to personally guarantee the development loan. They had previously contracted with a real estate developer named Nick Russell to build homes, subject to bank approval of the development loan. When the loan was approved, the arrangement became final.

The details were simple enough. Pearls would sell Russell up to three lots at a time. Russell would build and sell a home on each conveyed lot, and they would go on to the next set of lots. Bill and Agnes would pay off a pro rata portion of the development loan as each lot was sold to Russell. The rest was profit.

The parties planned that Russell would build an average of three homes per year, taking seven years to complete the project. Russell would purchase any lots not built upon at the end of seven years and the contract concluded.

The builder was reputable, having just completed the first phase of an extensive development of upscale condominiums in a nearby bedroom community. The first two units in Phase II sold quickly.

Bill and Agnes were counting on the net income from their subdivision to fund their retirement. What was left over would be bequeathed to their adult children. Bill and Agnes risked everything they owned to develop their property. Comfortable in the belief that they had secured their future, they sold their handsome home and moved to Texas.

Leonard Mercer was the president of a local bank holding the development loan and mortgage on the new subdivision, known as McKee Commons. By coincidence, Mercer had purchased one of the Phase I condominiums built by Nick Russell.

Mercer was a high strung and temperamental person, used to demanding and getting his own way. He felt his condominium purchased from Russell had construction shortcomings, and an ongoing series of disputes arose between Mercer and the builder. Russell could do nothing to please Mercer.

Most of Phase II in Russell's condominium project was behind Mercer's unit in Phase I and remained unsold. Phase I had sold out quickly, and Phase II sales were proceeding well until Mercer decided to take his dispute with Russell public. When prospects would visit Phase II units, they couldn't help but notice a large white sign with blue block letters in Mercer's window stating,

BEFORE YOU BUY, SEE ME FIRST!!
Or call XXX-XXXX

Sales of Phase II units slowed to only two closings following the initial two. Russell's cash flow dropped off a cliff. Never a large operator, he began to lag in his payments to crews, suppliers, and his lender. After finishing and selling only two houses in McKee Commons, he could no longer build in the development.

Bill and Agnes had no revenue coming in to make their loan payments, and after several months of delinquency their mortgage was foreclosed by Mercer's bank. As soon as the redemption period expired, McKee Commons would be sold at auction to satisfy the bank's debt.

Bill made the long flight to Iowa from Texas weak, ill, and confused. He'd aged considerably since I last saw him and looked like a defeated, broken man. Bill felt like a "dead beat" unable to make his loan payments. He was more embarrassed than angry. His hopes for retirement and his children's inheritance were gone.

Bill needed help, but I couldn't think of a way to provide it. It seemed that Nick Russell had a potential claim against Mercer for a species of libel called "false light invasion of privacy." This remedy is premised on the idea that when a private dispute is made public, and intentional or reckless falsehoods are spread which injure a person's private or business reputation, the libeled party may recover money damages. Mercer's "DON'T BUY" sign seemed to satisfy the requirements of the remedy. Russell also had a potential claim called, "tortious interference in prospective business advantage." This mouthful of words means that a person may be liable for wrongful damage to the business relationships of another.

But I didn't represent Nick Russell, and even if I did, a suit against Mercer likely wouldn't help Bill and Agnes. Their inability to meet their mortgage payments was an indirect result of Mercer's actions, but Mercer owed no duty to the McKee's or Pearls to refrain from ruining Russell.

Or did he? Were Mercer's actions a foreseeable result of his own bank's foreclosure of the Pearls/McKee mortgage? On the other hand, did Mercer have a free speech right that trumped Russell's right to the privacy of his business dispute? Did it matter to Bill and Agnes if he did or didn't?

None of this seemed to point the way toward any relief for the McKee family. Lawyer's ethics prohibited solicitation of Russell's legal business, in spite of present day billboards and commercials now cluttering our highways and TV screens. I couldn't advise Russell, whom I'd never met, of his potential claim nor suggest I could represent him. I could talk to him, though, as I could any other witness, about the Mercer situation. He agreed to meet me at my office.

Russell told me Mercer had been hounding him since the condominium closing. He showed me a signed statement from Mercer acknowledging that a standard list of construction problems, or "punch list," produced at the closing had been fixed to Mercer's satisfaction. The funds set aside from Russell's share of the closing proceeds to secure the adjustments had been released to Russell.

Still, at Mercer's insistence, Russell had gone back even after the punch list funds were released. Mercer was an important man around town, and Russell was anxious to please him. He corrected every tiny scratch in the woodwork Mercer complained about, even though Russell was sure the damage occurred when Mercer moved in. Mercer's decorator had a chandelier installed, and Russell was called to tighten the fixture to the ceiling after it slipped. Some of Mercer's sod died, and he expected Russell to replace it. As soon as one complaint was fixed, another sprang up to take its place. In short, Russell couldn't seem to satisfy Mercer under any circumstances.

Russell had the attitude I was looking for. He looked me in the eye, avoided no questions, and behaved in a way I found genuine and persuasive. I told him I was grateful for his time and information, and suggested he consult a good trial lawyer if he felt he was damaged by Mercer's actions. I could make a referral or two, but couldn't represent him. Finally, I said I hoped that he'd voluntarily cooperate if I found a way I could help the McKee's. He agreed.

When I considered filing suit on behalf of any Plaintiff, I tried to "circle the quarry" before deciding. I didn't know Leonard Mercer, but learned from a mutual acquaintance that his reputation was consistent with his behavior toward Nick Russell. Somehow I was comforted by this information, but it got me no closer to the goal line. I needed a legal means of redressing the foreclosure that, through no fault of Bill and Agnes, had ruined their lives and destroyed their children's inheritance.

I enjoyed legal research, but others in my firm were much better at it than I. In this case I reluctantly decided I should do it myself. Bill and Agnes were old friends, and I was personally invested in their case. And, I didn't feel I could ask an associate to spend endless hours on what I thought might prove a waste of time.

I spent parts of several days in a futile search for a remedy. Lawyers begin research from the premise that if a dispute with a particular fact pattern has occurred, something like it must have happened before. Then the problem would move into finding a similar instance in the case law and marshaling the ruling principle on behalf of the clients. While not exactly an original idea among lawyers, it often worked.

But my research wasn't turning up a similar case. Frustration mounted as my mediocre research skills failed me. Many hours over several days and most of a weekend had been lost without any progress.

As I sometimes did, I addressed all the law books and other texts in my law library, perhaps a hundred thousand dollars worth of resources, as I might deal with a child hiding in a cabinet. Frustration mounting, I said aloud, "I know you're in there somewhere!"

Close to giving up, I hit upon a little-used remedy called, "impairment of collateral." I felt the bank's board of directors and loan committee members might be faultless, but Mercer, by his behavior, had made foreclosure necessary.

Mercer wore two hats, after all. He acted on his own in harming Russell, and also acted in his capacity as chairman of the bank's board of directors in voting to approve foreclosure of the Pearls mortgage.

I knew I was out on a long and slender limb, but by this stage in my life I was familiar with the territory. I sued the bank and Mercer personally.

My first concern was to obtain an order staying the foreclosure sale until the case was resolved. Bill's children dug deep and posted the cash bond necessary to obtain the stay.

In unique cases, where the path to success or disaster is foggy, a lawyer wants to know as early in the representation as possible whether he's struck gold or iron pyrite. I suspected I'd struck gold when Mercer brought to Davenport the bank's lawyers from afar, not the local talent I was used to. Excellent counsel employed by the bank's home office in Des Moines proved worthy adversaries from a firm I knew well and respected.

Impairment of collateral is a rarely used claim. It's grounded in the principle that damage to the value of security pledged for the payment of a debt can be compensated if wrongful. I believed that Mercer, in a private dispute, unfairly injured Russell's reputation and business, which largely ended sales in Phase II of his condominium development. Mercer's "DON'T BUY" sign invited prospects to contact him. When they did, I surmised, they were treated to an unchallenged version of his construction disputes with Russell, tinged by Mercer's outright hatred of the builder.

The flow of revenue needed to keep Russell afloat from Phase II sales stopped. In turn, Russell's building activity in McKee Commons stopped, shutting off the stream of funds Pearls needed to pay Mercer's bank on the mortgage.

A strong circumstantial case could be made that the value of the McKee's lots was being injured, meaning the land securing Pearls' promise to pay, (the "collateral"), was "impaired". It couldn't be built upon in fulfillment of Russell's contract with Pearls. Without Russell's revenue stream Pearls could not survive and thrive.

Now the hard work began. Had Mercer been aware that his bank loaned development money to Bill and Agnes in the first place? Equally important, did he know about Russell's contract with Pearls? If we could prove these facts, we'd be taking a big step toward success. In carrying out his vendetta against Russell, we could infer, at least, that Mercer knowingly and recklessly harmed Bill and Agnes.

I drafted a request for production of documents and served it on Mercer's attorneys. We obtained the bank's entire loan file on the McKee mortgage including the original loan application, promissory notes, credit checks, the business plan for McKee Commons, a draft copy of Russell's proposed contract with Pearls, an appraisal of the development land, and the minutes of the meeting at which the bank's loan committee considered and approved the transaction. Finally, we also secured copies of all minutes of the loan committee and the board of directors meetings having any bearing on the decision to foreclose the Pearls mortgage.

We found the development loan was large enough to require approval by the bank's board of directors as a final step. We filed another request for copies of the minutes of the board's meeting at which the loan was approved as well.

It was clear from the results of this "paper discovery" that both the loan committee and the board of directors knew of Pearls' impending contract with Russell and the terms of the agreement. The details were fully explained in the business plan Bill and Agnes furnished the bank. Although the draft copy of the Pearls-Russell contract was unsigned, it was identical to the original and consistent with the business plan. Leonard Mercer himself, as chairman of the board of directors, presided over the meeting at which the board ratified the action of the loan committee in approving the loan.

The lawyers for the parties agreed on a round of depositions. Bill and Agnes were required to return to Davenport, as they knew they would. They held up well in spite of their age and assorted health problems. So did Nick Russell. Mercer, on the other hand, was combative, evasive, answered questions with questions, consulted often with his attorneys before answering even basic questions, and generally behaved like a spoiled child.

Mercer had a habit of opening his eyes wide at the end of his sentences, as if to emphasize what he had just said. Red faced and more than a little rude, he demanded not a glass of water, but a pitcher of water. He was unhappy that our office didn't provide ice.

This was a man used to getting his way. I asked Bill and Agnes to sit in the waiting room for the duration.

Perhaps the sharpest tool in the trial lawyer's toolbox is the leading question. The examining attorney may not ask leading questions of his own witness or independent witnesses under most circumstances, but may ask leading questions of opposing parties at will.

Why is the power to ask leading questions so valuable? First, the questioner can control the examination as non-leading questions do not permit. Depositions must be question-and-answer sessions, not conversations.

Second, an evasive or combative witness can be met with firmness or reciprocal combat when required. In addition to providing the means to maintain control, impetuous "blurt out" answers and other welcome candor can occasionally be the result.

The examiner must use considerable discipline in the questioning by not speaking over the witness, or unfairly speeding up the rhythm of the questions and answers. He must treat the witness with respect, while rigorously following a line of questions designed to illuminate, not intimidate. Seldom was the power to ask leading questions more helpful to me than in the Pearls lawsuit.

Mercer claimed he didn't recall the initial consideration of the Pearls loan proposal and volunteered that the amount was small enough that he may not have paid much attention. Mercer was making my closing argument for me. The borrowing may have been worth many times less than several million dollars to the bank, but it represented Bill and Agnes's entire future, and their children's inheritance as well.

As expected, Mercer had a long litany of complaints about his condominium unit and Nick Russell. By the end of the deposition it was clear that his "DON'T BUY" sign was not calculated to inform the public, but to harm Russell's business.

Mercer admitted he didn't take his complaints to the Better Business Bureau or the Quad Cities Builders Council. He didn't consider arbitration, mediation, or any other private means of dispute resolution. He never gave the viability of the McKee loan a thought, or if he did, he dismissed it. He was bent on ruining Nick Russell, pure and simple, and as publicly as possible.

Two reasons motivate lenders to attempt workouts of troubled loans before resorting to foreclosure. First, when a loan is rehabilitated the bank remains secured and payments in some amount continue. Both the bank and the borrower are better off.

Second, banks often stand in a fiduciary relationship with their borrowers. That is, when a borrower places trust and confidence in his bank, the bank owes a high duty to protect him from unreasonable harm. As inexperienced and unsophisticated borrowers, Bill and Agnes were strong candidates for a finding by the court that they stood in a fiduciary relationship with Mercer's bank.

Mercer was obviously a strong and influential leader. If he steered the board toward foreclosure without advising the board members of his personal vendetta and its likely effect on the McKee enterprise, any chance to save the Russell-McKee business relationship would be lost. If Mercer's conflict of interest was unknown to everyone else on the board, there was no chance the board would push back against Mercer, convincing him to take down his sign, and reinvigorating sales in Russell's condominium project. The board's ignorance of the dispute would be fatal to the McKee Commons project.

The colloquy between us was strained but enlightening. JDS: Mr. Mercer, you've testified that you had your differences with Nick Russell over the condominium you purchased from him, correct?

WITNESS: Yes, I have so testified.

JDS: And you understood that the sign in your window and your discussions with people who contacted you might be discourage them from buying from Russell, right?

WITNESS: I don't recall anybody contacting me.

JDS: For the record, I move to strike that answer as unresponsive. Miss reporter, will you read the question back?

(REPORTER COMPLIES)

WITNESS: I don't know.

JDS: (Continuing): Your sign was in your window for almost eight months. We've established that, correct?

WITNESS: That's correct.

JDS: And in that entire period you can't remember anyone contacting you in response to the invitation presented on your sign?

WITNESS: No.

JDS: Are you testifying under oath that no one ever contacted you in response to that sign?

WITNESS: No, I just don't recall.

JDS: Really?

MR MILLER: Object...

WITNESS: Really.

MR. MILLER: ...to the question as argumentative, and ask for the record that my objection precede the response.

JDS: That's fine. (Continuing) Do you know of any other likely reason Phase II sales fell off the table after Phase I sold so well? Sold out, in fact, except for the display model??

WITNESS: That's none of my business.

JDS: And speaking of the display model, your sign could be seen from the walkway leading from the sales office to the model, correct?

WITNESS: I suppose so.

JDS: And two units of Phase II sold quickly, before you put up your sign, correct?

WITNESS: I have no way of knowing that, and I just told you it was none of my business.

JDS: Well, you made it your business by putting the sign in your window, didn't you?

WITNESS: I was trying to warn people.

JDS: Would you agree that, giving you the benefit of the doubt, even if nobody contacted you, prospects seeing your sign might still be discouraged from buying a unit in Phase II?

WITNESS: That would be impossible to know. Speculation.

JDS: Well, wasn't that your whole point?

WITNESS: My warning just meant that people should decide for themselves.

JDS: Well, sure, who else would be in a position to decide for them?

MR. MILLER: Counsel, for the record, that's argumentative and objected to for that reason. (To the witness) You may answer if you can. The judge will rule on the objection at a later time.

WITNESS: I don't know how to answer that.

JDS: Fair enough. Let's turn to your dealings as your bank's chairman of the board for a moment. Did you ever mention your personal issues with Russell to the board?

WITNESS: No.

JDS: Did you ever mention your personal issues with Russell to any member of the board outside of a meeting?

WITNESS: Not that I remember.

JDS: In fact, the board minutes of the meeting in which foreclosure was approved don't reflect any mention of your dispute?

WITNESS: No, but minutes don't reflect everything that went on.

JDS: Well, something as important as your personal conflict of interest would be important enough to be recorded in the minutes, wouldn't it?

WITNESS: There was no conflict. I didn't keep the minutes and I wouldn't know. Not an issue.

JDS: Mr. Mercer, did it ever occur to you to explain to your board that a possible reason for the McKee/Pearls loan delinquency was your dispute with Nick, and your active discouragement of potential buyers from investing in his project?

WITNESS: (To the reporter) Would you read that back?

JDS: That's fine. (Reporter complies.)

WITNESS: No, it had no bearing whatsoever.

JDS: Did you ever think about abstaining from voting for foreclosure in light of your conflict of interest?

WITNESS: I had no conflict. The foreclosure was about McKee's failure to pay, not Russell.

JDS: But you knew Russell was responsible to McKee's for their cash flow to pay your bank's mortgage, right?

WITNESS: I knew no such thing.

JDS: Well, let's look at Mercer Deposition Exhibit 14 once more, sir. That's the minutes of the meeting when your board approved the Pearls/McKee development loan. You concede that you attended that board meeting, right?

WITNESS: I know where you're going with this. It shows I attended but I have no recollection. That's almost two years ago.

JDS: To be clear, you attended, and the business plan showing the Pearls/McKee construction contract with Nick Russell and even a draft copy of the contract itself was discussed and approved along with the development loan, correct?

WITNESS: It shows that, but I have no recollection.

JDS: And just to be clear, you voted to approve the loan committee's decision to foreclose the McKee/Pearls mortgage almost two years later, didn't you?

WITNESS: That's correct.

JDS: You did not abstain?

WITNESS: I did not abstain.

JDS: And when a decision to foreclose is being considered, the original loan file is carefully reviewed beforehand, isn't it?

WITNESS: Somebody reviews it. Not me.

JDS: And the original loan file clearly shows Nick Russell as the builder for Pearls, Inc., doesn't it?

WITNESS: Yes.

JDS: Let me ask you a hypothetical question. And I'll give you the benefit of the doubt that you don't remember Russell being McKee's builder. If you had reviewed that file and found out Russell was the builder, would you have advised your board of your dispute with Nick and how you were dealing with it?

WITNESS: I doubt it.

JDS: Because?

WITNESS: It was a private matter.

JDS: And to recap, you didn't tell anyone on your board or any member of the loan committee about your personal dispute with the source of the McKee funds to pay your bank's mortgage, which was Nick Russell?

WITNESS: No, and I saw absolutely no reason to. It was a private matter, and I didn't recall the connection.

JDS: Well Mr. Mercer, once again, you made it public with your sign, didn't you?

WITNESS: I was trying to be helpful to potential buyers, but it had no bearing on the bank's decisions.

JDS: So it was okay for the public to know about your dispute with Russell, but not the bank's board?

WITNESS: That's right.

JDS: Why not? *[I took a big chance with this question. A lawyer should never ask a "why" question unless he knows the answer. And I didn't.]*

WITNESS: Russell's success in Phase II didn't matter. There should have been enough cash flow to pay down the McKee loan, regardless of Russell's sales problems with his other project.

JDS: Well, how would you know that?

WITNESS: Russell must have had other income from other projects to buy lots with and construct houses, or he could borrow it.

JDS: How do you know that?

WITNESS. I assume so.

JDS: Really?

WITNESS: Yes.

JDS: From Bill and Agnes' point of view, they did pay off a pro rata share of the development loan for the first three lots sold to Russell, right?

WITNESS: Yes.

JDS: And Russell built on two of them and promptly sold the houses?

WITNESS: I understand that.

JDS: And your sign went up in your window in about mid-August, right?

WITNESS: I don't know exactly when it went up.

JDS: Sir, you were present for Nick Russell's deposition yesterday. You heard him say that his sales dried up in September, after your sign went up in August, right?

WITNESS: He also said two sales happened afterwards.

JDS: And you also heard him say those sales were already in the pipeline before your sign went in your window, correct?

WITNESS: I have no way of confirming that.

JDS: Listen to the question. You heard Nick Russell testify under oath at his deposition that the two Phase II condominium sales that closed after your sign went up were in the pipeline beforehand, right?

WITNESS: I said I heard that, but I can't confirm it.

JDS: Mr. Mercer, you've testified that you have a business degree. You've testified that you have been involved with finance all your professional life. You can understand that any net profit Russell made on the two houses he sold in McKee Commons would almost certainly have to go towards his construction loan that was seriously delinquent on Phase II due to lack of sales, right?

WITNESS: That was none of my business.

JDS: Well, we've talked about that. You can surely imagine that Russell was financially stressed by his Phase II loan delinquency and had no cash or borrowing power to proceed in McKee Commons?

WITNESS: No, I don't know that at all.

JDS: Well, he said so in his deposition, under oath. You were there. Do you have any reason to doubt it?

WITNESS: I'm skeptical, let's put it that way.

JDS: And I guess you accept zero responsibility for the fall-off in sales of Phase II condos?

WITNESS: Absolutely.

JDS: Sir, I've never been on a bank board or served on a loan committee. But I would think, just as a matter of normal human behavior, that someone in that meeting would ask something like, "What's the matter with this Pearls loan? Why aren't payments being made? Two homes were built, regular payments were made, and then the well dried up. Why? Is foreclosure inevitable, and if so, why?" Did anyone ask those questions?

WITNESS: Not that I remember.

JDS: You didn't ask those questions, did you?

WITNESS: No.

JDS: Mr. Mercer, why did you take your sign out of your window?

WITNESS: I don't remember. I don't think I had a particular reason.

JDS: You took your sign out of your window because it had done its work, didn't you? You had succeeded in ruining Nick Russell?

WITNESS: That's highly offensive and preposterous.

JDS: Mr. Mercer, would you agree with me that you had knowledge no other member of the loan committee and no other member of your board had? You knew why Russell wasn't selling units in Phase II, and you had reason to know why Bill and Agnes couldn't make their loan payments to your bank, didn't you?

WITNESS: I knew no such thing.

JDS: You said a few minutes ago, and I'm paraphrasing here, your lawyer will correct me if I'm wrong, that the McKee mortgage stood alone, and didn't depend on Russell's sales in Phase II for revenue to pay your bank's mortgage. Is that what you said?

WITNESS: Pretty much.

JDS: Well, if Russell didn't have any other cash coming in, or have a pile of money in the bank, where were the funds supposed to come from?

WITNESS: From lot sales.

JDS: Well, Russell couldn't build in McKee Commons if he couldn't sell Phase II units, right?

WITNESS: I didn't know that.

JDS: To correct you slightly, you knew when the loan was being considered that Russell and McKee's had contracted together, but you just forgot?

WITNESS: I did forget. And McKee's could've broken their contract with Russell and hired another builder.

JDS: Have you read Russell's contract with McKee's?

WITNESS: No.

JDS: Then you aren't aware of the restrictions and penalties that might benefit Russell if Bill and Agnes tried to void the contract?

WITNESS: I haven't read the contract.

JDS: Would you like to?

WITNESS: I'm not a lawyer. And furthermore, any penalties or consequences of breaking the contract were irrelevant.

JDS: Well, the bank approved it when the loan was made and a copy has been in your bank's file ever since. You knew that, right?

WITNESS: I'm not sure anyone paid any attention to it.

JDS: Mr. Mercer, when did you first become aware that the Pearls mortgage was running behind on payments?

WITNESS: I think it was brought to my attention around ninety days into delinquency. That's standard.

JDS: When you learned of the delinquency, did you wonder why? Did it dawn on you...did any light bulb go off that no payments were coming in because Nick Russell was McKee's builder and wasn't selling units in Phase II?

WITNESS: No.

JDS: Mr. Mercer, take a look at Mercer deposition exhibit 26. What is it?

WITNESS: It's a memo from the loan committee to the board.

JDS: I'll tell you that this memo was contained in the file your lawyers produced to us in response to our subpoena. Read along with me where I've highlighted in yellow: "Nick Russell is the contractor on the project. He has not begun a house since finishing the second one in June." Did I read that correctly?

WITNESS: Yes.

JDS: Have you seen that before?

WITNESS: My lawyers showed it to me.

JDS: When?

WITNESS: Last week in Des Moines.

JDS: Do you remember ever seeing it before then?

WITNESS: No.

JDS: Do you have any idea how this memo could be directed to the attention of the board without coming to your individual attention?

WITNESS: No, but I assure you, it happened.

JDS: And you're still saying that neither you nor anyone on your board paid any attention to why Russell hadn't built a third house in McKee Commons or even four, and coincidentally the McKee loan was in arrears?

WITNESS: Yes, sir, I am.

Following Mercer's deposition, I privately informed his counsel that I planned to seek an amendment to the Complaint to add a count pleading punitive damages, as I thought his deposition provided a factual basis for it. Punitive damages can be thought of as civil punishment for wrongdoing, and to serve as an example to others. I thought Mercer's claim that he couldn't remember anyone responding to his sign was plainly untrue, and told his lawyers so.

I also told them it seemed impossible that Mercer didn't know about the loan committee's memo to the board noting Russell was McKee's builder. I advised them that the rest of the board would be answering similar questions under oath shortly. It was almost inconceivable that Mercer forgot about Russell's contract with McKee's and Pearls, but even if he did, the memo would remind him. And he kept silent.

Addressing Mercer's "DON'T BUY" sign, I noted most prospects go house hunting on weekends. Prospects are always invited to see the furnished and decorated model, and Mercer's sign was hard to miss. He would likely be home on most weekends. After seeing his sign, and imagining myself as a prospect interested in buying, I would have been foolish not to knock on his door, or at least call him at the number shown on his sign. No vivid imagination was required to guess what Mercer would say to prospects, and what the effect might be.

Finally, I told them I suspected both that the bank owed a fiduciary duty to the McKee's, owing to their trust and confidence in the bank, and the bank breached their duty.

It soon appeared perhaps Mercer's lawyers didn't believe him any more than I did. A settlement was reached before I had a chance to amend the suit. The bank dropped the foreclosure, forgave the entire loan balance, released the development mortgage, restored the McKee's credit rating, and paid my attorney's fees and court costs.

With the loan forgiven and the mortgage released, Bill and Agnes resumed development of McKee Commons with another builder. Now, when a lot was sold in McKee Commons, Bill and Agnes could pocket the entire proceeds without bank loan payments coming off the top.

Nick Russell waived his rights under the Pearls contract and slowly worked his way out of his financial problems. Bill died of heart failure in the following year. I hope his children, his "pearls," knew how much he and Aggie went through for them.

VI
Learning by Losing

Nothing except a battle lost can be half so melancholy as a battle won.
    -Lord Wellington

Pride goeth before a fall.
    -Proverbs 16:18

Not everything I did turned out well. It's a terrible blow to absorb losing a case you thought you would win, and should win. It is harder still to call the client and report the bad news.

Grain Processing Company (GPC) does just what the name describes. It buys wheat, corn, and a few other grains and produces various products, including alcohol for human consumption. Huge barges full of alcohol are sent down the Mississippi to Tennessee for use by distilleries in that state and in Kentucky. I was surprised to learn that alcohol is injected into many liquor products, not fermented and distilled into them. A GPC alcohol-laden barge once sank just south of Muscatine on its way to Tennessee, and the locals joked that thousands of catfish had big, drunken smiles on their faces.

One of GPC's main businesses is separating gluten from wheat. It's used in animal feeds and other products. Gluten comes out of the processing facility to a covered loading area where it's dropped into huge piles. Then it's pushed along the floor by end loader to a grated system about 100 feet long where it falls about 18" through a metal grate into a trough. It's then transported by screw auger to trucks waiting to carry it to animal feed manufacturers.

Jim Phillips hauled gluten as a private trucker and delivered it to an animal feed manufacturer. He was a frequent visitor to the plant. A waiting area was provided for drivers, and Phillips usually hung out there while the system loaded his truck.

One day the auger wasn't filling Jim's truck fast enough to suit him. The floor workers were on break. Phillips decided to enter the processing area and check the auger lines, which could be seen through the metal grating in the loading floor. He looked around and didn't see anything wrong. He picked up a push broom and began pushing gluten into the auger line from a large pile nearby.

At some point Phillips stepped on a grate, which came loose, dropping his left leg into the moving auger. He later said he felt his toes torn off, and nothing after that. The auger chewed Phillips' leg up to the hip, and even tore off part of his scrotum before he was pulled free.

Phillips sued GPC for failure to warn him of an unsafe condition, failure to inspect, discover, and remedy an unsafe condition, failure to provide a safe place to work, and various other breaches of due care. His lawyer hired an expert witness, who decided that a sensor with a kill switch should have been installed that would interrupt the power to the auger if undue stress were placed on the machinery. He also faulted the grate system as badly designed and unsafe.

Phillips' lawyer was a fellow I knew well. In fact, I'd beaten him several times and held his trial skills in low regard. He had a terrible nasal voice, and looked like a bespectacled stork. The shoulders of his dark blue suits were often a snowfall of dandruff issuing from his curly-permed head. The reader might take from this description that I didn't like him. I actually did. He was a decent guy just trying to do his job.

His professional skills were even less impressive. His slow, deliberate, and repetitive style caused jurors to move around in their seats and grow impatient with every unbroken silence while he looked at his notes between agonizingly complex questions. I advised GPC and its insurer that a defense verdict was likely.

I felt our defenses were powerful, but rather technical. First, Phillips was permitted on the premises, but not the location where he was injured. He was invited to the drivers' waiting area but not into the work area. This absolves the company from fault if the jury finds he's technically a trespasser in the area where he was injured, and therefore not entitled to a "safe place to work".

Second, Phillips qualified under the law as an "officious inter-loper." This obscure term applies when a person, unqualified and uninvited, tries to help in an activity in which he has no business. He has no right to complain about damages suffered when he elbows his way into someone else's responsibilities. The courts hold that he's owed no duty. A claim exists where there's a duty to another, a negligent breach of that duty, and damages. Phillips, by undertaking the gluten-sweeping responsibility of a GPC employee, was arguably both a trespasser and an officious interloper.

Third, Phillips was a rather unpleasant, know-it-all type, from my perspective. I believed that in spite of his terrible injuries the jury would do the right thing and reluctantly conclude Phillips wasn't entitled to a verdict.

Boy, was I wrong. The jury returned what was then the largest single verdict ever awarded in Muscatine County. In defense of our claim that he entered a non-permitted area Phillips said he'd done the same thing on another occasion while within view of the shop foreman, without complaint. Evidently, the jury believed Phillips and not the foreman, who denied it.

My "record" held up for years, and I was the butt of frequent kidding by my brethren at the bar. Thankfully, a larger verdict eventually took me off the hook.

I should have taken the advice of an experienced old trial lawyer who told me, "You take the law and I'll take the facts and I'll beat you every time." In other words, an advantage in a technical legal defense is often greatly outweighed by an advantage on the other side in the fact issues of the case. I couldn't overcome the natural human sympathy the jury felt for Phillips and his wife as contrasted with my legal defenses, whatever merit they might have had. I now believe I was too smug in relying on legal technicalities to win, and should have developed a more realistic defense strategy better emphasizing a more persuasive case on the facts. Harder to admit is that my opponent beat me in the biggest case of his career, and up to that time, mine as well.

Trying every case should be a learning experience. One of our clients specialized in insuring county and city governments. The reader might be surprised at the number of people who fall down on city sidewalks and sue for injuries. I was. Consequently, I spent the first several years of my career handling a great many slip and fall defenses for eastern Iowa cities great and small.

I developed a routine for defending these claims and had a string of victories prompting me to think of myself as surely the next Perry Mason. I could always find evidence that the plaintiff wasn't keeping a proper lookout for open and obvious conditions, or failed to take an alternate safe route, or wasn't wearing footwear appropriate to conditions, or assumed the risk of injury despite knowledge of a dangerous walking surface. Moreover, Midwest juries seem to understand that rough and slippery snow and ice will always be present to some extent in that latitude, and perfect sidewalks may exist in heaven, but they're nowhere to be found in Dubuque.

These trials became so routine that for a time I became lazy. I didn't have the challenge of new situations demanding the creativity I needed to keep me fresh.

In the mid-seventies I was assigned the defense of a case involving a construction worker who had fallen to his death from a roof several stories high. The case had some aspects of a slip and fall claim, I thought, and I counted on my tried and true strategies to win.

The facts were simple, but gruesome. A large manufacturing plant hired an outside industrial construction contractor to build an addition onto an existing building. To reach the work area, the construction workers had to walk across a corrugated roof several stories above a railroad siding. Due to age and deposits of soot and other products of the plant, the roof looked like a typical gray corrugated metal roof. It was actually made of Transite, a Johns-Manville asbestos product much lighter than metal, but unsuitable for weight-bearing.

The construction company's employees attended safety meetings before beginning the job, and every Monday before the work week began. Mitch Conrad was present at the meetings, as required. According to his fellow workers, the Transite roof was discussed, and workers were warned to follow the rivet lines along the roof to the work site. The rivets fastened the Transite to heavy steel framing, pointing the way to a safe path.

After several days on the job, Mr. Conrad was sent back to the tool area on an errand. He walked back safely, mounted a catwalk, and fetched a needed tool. He returned across the catwalk and vaulted over the railing onto the roof.

Conrad hit the roof where no steel frame members would support him. The Transite shattered under his weight. He fell through the roof to the railroad tracks several stories below. Conrad was killed instantly when his head struck the tracks. His estate and widow brought a civil suit against the factory owner, claiming failure to warn of an unsafe condition, failure to provide a safe place to work, and other claims of fault.

I developed my defense strategy along the lines of my successful slip and fall cases. Mr. Conrad knew of the safety issue and must have momentarily forgotten the hazard when he vaulted over the catwalk railing.

A property owner may either warn of an unsafe condition or make the condition safe. When an invitee is warned, all duties are fulfilled. What could be simpler? The warnings given at the contractor's safety meetings carried the same legal weight as if given by the factory owner.

Things went well until I discovered too late that there were no minutes of the relevant safety meetings. The Occupational Safety and Health Act (OSHA) required that minutes be taken and preserved, but none could be found. Although hearsay, the missing minutes would have been admitted into evidence as a business record.

To make matters worse, the person who'd given the safety meetings had died. Oral testimony from co-workers relating what he'd said about the roof would be inadmissible hearsay. OSHA confirmed the safety meetings took place, but the company's reports didn't include the minutes themselves. I had to face the fact that I couldn't prove the contents of the safety meetings.

I had some circumstantial evidence that Conrad must have known about the hazard because, obviously, on several previous trips to and from the work site he never fell through the roof. But I didn't have sufficient evidence that he always walked along the rivet lines. Conrad was a small man and may not have fallen through the roof just in the act of walking off the rivet lines. But landing on the roof after jumping over the railing added so much force to the Transite that he was a goner for sure.

The hard truth was that we were certain Conrad was warned of the roof condition and instructed on how to walk on it. But we couldn't prove it.

After confidently predicting victory to my client for almost two years, I had to back off and recommend settlement. We settled on a compromise basis, somewhat favorably for my client.

I believe that if I'd been assigned that defense several years later in my career, I would have seen the strategy differently and quite distinct from the principles that had served me well in slip and fall defenses. The danger on the roof was not apparent, as ice on a sidewalk is. A sign at the catwalk would have been easy to post, and would have reminded workers daily of the hidden danger. And if I'd understood the proof problems in the case at the outset, a settlement recommendation might have overcome my trial instincts.

The case also taught me something I suppose most people know intuitively: assemble and master the facts as early as possible. Years of time and thousands of dollars in fees could have been saved if I'd discovered the absence of the safety meeting notes earlier.

Eldon McCracken was a hobo, with no visible means of support. He looked about seventy years old, but was in his late fifties, with wrinkled, leathery skin, a stubbly beard and few remaining teeth. Eldon lived year 'round in a derelict boxcar on a remote Rock Island Railroad siding along Nahant Marsh, southwest of town. He'd installed a cook stove and a rudimentary commode, and bothered no one. The boxcar never went anywhere, held captive on an unused spur.

Eldon's sole diversion was a weekly trek to Bill's Bull Pen, a local strip joint in an industrial area near the tracks where Eldon would watch the girls and proceed to become drunk out of his mind. He was a fixture at the club, often loudly commenting on the caliber of the local dancing talent.

One Monday morning around 11:00, Bill opened up for the week. As he set up chairs and polished the bar, he heard a muffled pounding coming from the basement. He walked to the basement stairs, unlocked the door, and at the foot of the stairs was Eldon, squinting up into the light. His arm was badly broken at the elbow, but no other injuries were apparent beyond the usual bumps and bruises. Bill took Eldon to the hospital where his arm was set. Bill's business insurance paid Eldon's bills.

At first, Eldon professed not to remember what happened. He soon went to a lawyer and had total recall. Late that Saturday evening, Eldon said that he made his way toward the restroom, which he'd visited many times before. The basement door was located between the men's and ladies rooms, each of which was well marked.

The basement door had no marking on it at all. It was kept unlocked during business hours to afford easy access to cases of beer kept in the basement. Eldon mistook the basement door for the men's room door, took a step forward in the dark, and tumbled down the stairs, breaking his arm.

Confused and most likely drunk, he sat on the floor at the bottom of the stairs, calling for help. The raucous music, cheering, and general commotion upstairs prevented anyone from hearing Eldon. Nobody missed him. A barmaid saw the basement door open and simply closed it, not realizing what happened.

When closing time arrived, the basement door was locked and the business shut down. By that time Eldon had either passed out or fallen asleep. When he awoke and climbed the stairs, he found himself locked in for the night. The tavern was closed on Sunday, so Eldon was Bill's unintended guest for the Sabbath as well.

Eldon's lawyer sued. He claimed Bill was negligent in leaving the basement door unmarked and unlocked, and in failing to have the basement stairs lit during business hours. In response, I alleged that Eldon had actual knowledge of where the men's room was, owing to his numerous visits there on past occasions. He failed to pay attention to where he was going, and he was intoxicated.

The latter defense is easy to understand. If an individual voluntarily dulls his senses and judgment by becoming intoxicated and is later injured while under the influence, he can't recover for his injuries if the intoxication played a part in causing the accident.

We went to trial. Eldon's lawyer proved inexperienced, but brought an enthusiasm and verve to the case that I didn't expect. He pointed out there was no proof Eldon was drunk at the time he fell.

I admitted that was true, because whatever alcohol was in his system on Saturday night had metabolized by Monday morning when his blood was drawn at the hospital. Rather, I argued a principle called "custom and practice." Eldon was usually in our tavern on Friday or Saturday nights, and sometimes both. He invariably stayed until closing time, drinking steadily and exhibiting unmistakable signs of intoxication. There was plenty of evidence in the record from other regulars to support this claim. By inference, Eldon was probably intoxicated, as usual, when he fell down the stairs.

Eldon's lawyer countered that if Eldon was indeed drunk, it was Bill who sold him the beer in the first place. It's hard to claim innocence due to another's intoxication when you yourself profited from the drinking.

The jury returned a verdict of $87,000 for Eldon's injury. That was a great deal of money for a broken arm in the mid-1980's, and probably still is. A judge later reduced the award by $30,000, but I was still stung.

The hard lessons I learned in Eldon's case and the GPC debacle were, first, never underestimate the power and natural jury appeal of the underdog, or his lawyer, either. Second, while educated guesses may often be right, you can never tell what a jury is going to do.

VII

Heard Any Good Lawyer Jokes?

Sometimes trials lend comic relief to the hard business of jury work. In a rear end collision trial sometime in the 1970's, a locally notorious doctor testified in support of the plaintiff's complaints of neck injuries.

The presiding judge was *sui generis,* or, one of a kind. She was the first female judge appointed to the state district court and quite confident of her abilities as a judge, her knowledge of the law, and the way the world ought to be in general. After many motion hearings before her, trials to the bench, jury trials and other matters, I developed the opinion that no matter how ably my opponent and I argued our positions, this judge could be counted upon to discover and adopt a third view.

She wasn't shy about offering her opinions in front of juries or anyone else within earshot. One wise lawyer used to say she was "often wrong, but never in doubt." She was also among the judges most reversed by the Iowa Supreme Court.

The doctor was on a roll. He offered his opinion that the plaintiff had developed bony spurs in her neck as a consequence of arthritis brought on by the accident. The spurring was indeed visible on X-ray, but doubtfully caused by the accident because spurring normally takes several years to develop. He further testified that he was able to hear a crackling noise in her neck when the plaintiff turned her head from side to side. This condition, called crepitus, often accompanies spurring. Then, the doctor went too far. He testified that crepitus is always evidence of pain.

The judge had heard enough. In her best imitation of Judge Judy, she leaned over toward the physician, whom she had cross-examined many times herself as a lawyer. Glaring at him, she yelled, "Oh, yeah? Come up here and listen to this!" at which time she proceeded to shake her head vigorously from side to side.

Ordinarily, such an interjection into a jury trial by the judge would have resulted in a motion for mistrial, but the plaintiff's lawyer was so dumbstruck by her explosive comments that he just went on.

―――――――――

A friend related another story characteristic of this judge. At the conclusion of a hard fought trial she sent the jury out of the courtroom to begin deliberations. Then, in front of the clients on both sides, she praised my friend's young and rather smarmy opponent to the skies. He had done magnificently, she rhapsodized, and had all the talents of a great trial lawyer. She said he had a wonderful future as an advocate, and predicted a generous verdict for him and his client.

"And you," she glared at my friend, a bright and competent lawyer who had defended hundreds of cases, "You need to go back to law school!"

Guess who won?

―――――――――

Fort Madison, Iowa is another Mississippi River town where I tried many cases. George Reynolds, a great lawyer with a terrific sense of humor, lived there. His easygoing nature and courtesy always made it a pleasure to deal with him on the opposing side.

George had a big heart and had a hard time turning down weak cases. One example involved a woman who went shopping for Thanksgiving dinner. She claimed she lifted a big frozen turkey out of the supermarket's freezer case and started to put it in her shopping cart. She said the plastic carrying handle fastened to the turkey either broke or became detached from the turkey. The big gobbler fell on her foot, breaking several bones.

She then gathered the turkey off the floor, put it in her cart, finished her shopping, limped to the check out aisle, and bought the bird along with her other groceries. She didn't mention the accident to the check out girl, the store manager, or anyone.

I used procedural means to limit the proof in the case. Essentially a products liability claim, it was necessary to have the carrying handle and its attachment to the turkey available so both sides could inspect and test them to try to determine the cause of the failure, if indeed it happened at all. For all we knew, the plaintiff may well have dropped the turkey on her foot without any defect she could blame on the frozen fowl or the handle. She couldn't produce the handle. And, of course, the turkey was long gone. Other than her word, she had no evidence.

Even worse, if the defense is prevented by the act of the plaintiff from an opportunity to independently inspect and test an allegedly defective product, a doctrine called "spoliation of evidence" (not "spoilation") virtually guarantees that the plaintiff won't be able to prove her case. The claim was dismissed for lack of evidence.

This was the only case in my experience where the plaintiff bought the object that had already injured her, took it home, and ate the evidence. George said ruefully, "I'm often accused of taking turkey cases, but this time it's true!

———

I learned early to beware of co-defendants. Defending a claim with multiple defendants and involving multiple lawyers can muddle a trial strategy. Mixed messages, arguments among lawyers on the same side of the case, and much intramural finger pointing usually works to the plaintiff's advantage. Sometimes, however, a co-defendant provides a delicious and unforgettable moment.

Such a moment came in a trial involving a three-car collision. I represented one defendant, and a well-known but rather pompous lawyer from an even more pompous firm represented the other.

The plaintiff had introduced her kitchen calendar to refresh her recollection and provide proof supporting her visits to her doctors and a physical therapist. The plaintiff's lawyer and I both knew that the other defendant's lawyer was losing his case. He began taking chances in hopes of striking gold in cross-examination. He violated the old rule: *Never ask a question unless you know the answer.*

LAWYER: Mrs. Wilson, I believe you testified on direct that you were unable to sit for long periods of time without pain and discomfort?

WITNESS: Yes, that's true.

LAWYER: For example, you said under oath that it's hard for you to sit through a movie in a theater?

WITNESS: Yes.

LAWYER: And you further testified that you were unable to sit in the car for long trips without discomfort?

WITNESS: Yes.

LAWYER: Well, here, Mrs. Wilson, in the month of September your calendar shows you went to Minnesota, doesn't it?

WITNESS: No.

LAWYER, (plowing forward): And in October, you again show a trip to Minnesota, isn't that true?

WITNESS: No, sir.

LAWYER, (digging his grave deeper): And again in November, here's another trip to Minnesota, correct?

WITNESS: No, sir.

LAWYER: And December too, right?

WITNESS: No.

LAWYER: Well it says MN on each of these months, doesn't it?

WITNESS: (demurely) Sir, that stands for Mother Nature.

———

Another moment occurred not in the courtroom, but in a Scott County Bar Association meeting. An elderly lawyer with the improbable (and real) name of Waldo Wissler rose to speak following the business meeting. Waldo was a real character who could often be seen riding his ancient bike to his office, rain or shine. On this occasion Waldo held forth on the great pleasure he used get from attending the annual bar outing. Why weren't we holding these events anymore? Employing rhetorical flourishes and gestures from a bygone era, Waldo allowed that he greatly missed these opportunities for collegiality, camaraderie, and the enjoyment that comes from playing a round of golf, breaking bread, and partaking of good food and drink with his fellow barristers.

During this disquisition he was interrupted by several of our brethren, who cried, "Waldo, Waldo, we had the bar outing at the country club last month!"

"Oh," Waldo replied. "Was I there?"

A classic found in a reported case from many years ago involved a construction accident. The injured party was asked to explain what happened. The answer has entertained lawyers and others for many years.

Because we were done for the day, we commenced to bring our materials down from the scaffold. The foreman told me to lower the barrel of nails from the third floor using the block and tackle we raised our tools etc. with. I soon found out the barrel was heavier than me. Still holding the rope, I was pulled up toward the scaffold very fast. The barrel struck my head as it went by the other way. I jammed my fingers in the wheel when I arrived at the top, but I held on.

The barrel bottom broke when it hit the ground, scattering nails all over. I was now heavier than the barrel. I went down as the barrel went up. It struck my left leg as it went by. I landed on the nails from the barrel, cutting my backside and breaking my hip. Then I lost my head and let go of the rope. The barrel came down and struck me on the head and shoulders, knocking me out. Then it was over.

Part of the local lore involved my mentor, Arthur Middleton, Sr. For many years before Arthur, Jr. joined him, Mr. Middleton practiced in partnership with a lawyer who enjoyed a nip or two from the bottle as much as Arthur did. Both of Scottish extraction, they would often stroll to a nearby tavern after work and enjoy a couple of pleasant hours together.

One evening Mr. Middleton was at home when he received a phone call from his partner. He'd been arrested and charged with drunk driving. Could Arthur come down and bail him out? Of course he could.

Arthur drove downtown to the jail with his checkbook, ready to free his tipsy comrade. Instead, noticing a strong odor of alcohol and an unsteady gait, the police arrested Arthur for public intoxication and OWI, and placed him in the same holding cell with his partner.

——— ———

Of course, everyone has their favorite lawyer jokes, and I have my personal favorites as well.

A doctor, an engineer, and a lawyer were on a long flight and talked into the night about the merits of their respective professions. They got to wondering which of the three was the earliest field of endeavor.

The physician noted that God took a rib from Adam and made Eve. This miracle was the first surgical procedure, and surely meant that medicine was the oldest profession.

The engineer replied that no, God did something before that. He created the earth, the moon, the stars and the entire universe, out of chaos! That was the first, and not incidentally, the greatest engineering achievement ever. Therefore, he smugly concluded, engineering was the oldest profession.

The doctor and the engineer looked at the lawyer, and the lawyer looked at them and said, "Well, who do you think created the chaos?"

——— ———

Juries in agricultural states like Iowa often hear claims generically called "cow in the road" cases. With hundreds of thousands of animals in rural areas, automobiles occasionally crash into cows, horses, and pigs that find their way out of confinement somehow. Collisions with these large animals can cause serious injury and even death. Legislatures and courts have responded to the problem by requiring farmers to assume liability for faulty fences and gates that allow their animals to escape onto the highway.

Late one Fourth of July evening an elderly couple was driving home from Monticello, Iowa where they'd attended a fireworks display with their grandson. An entire herd of dairy cows had ambled out of an adjacent barnyard due to a faulty gate. Their car struck a cow at full speed, killing the animal and destroying the automobile. The car's battery was ripped away and the lights went out.

The grandfather got out to see what happened. A car coming from the other direction saw the mess and stopped in the oncoming lane, facing toward the front of the destroyed vehicle. Trying to be helpful, he put his headlights on high beam to warn other motorists and provide a better light source for the grandfather.

Marlene Olson and her husband were a few miles behind the car that struck the cow, driving home from the same fireworks display. Being unable to see the unlit dark blue car stopped in the road, and with the bright headlights of the other car in their eyes, they smashed into the stalled car from behind, pushing it into the grandfather and killing him. His grandson was injured and ultimately lost a kidney. The grandmother and the Olson's were uninjured.

The grandfather's estate, the grandmother, and the grandson's guardian all brought suit against the farmer and Marlene Olson. The grandfather's estate was also named as a defendant in the grandson's suit for injuries. I defended Marlene Olson in Delaware County District Court.

The trial took about a week. It had been a long week. Many stops and starts for legal and procedural issues drew the trial out. The heat in my motel room sputtered for a night or two and finally quit for good. I had to move out the next morning to a different motel. The kindly but elderly judge called me, "Mr. Studebaker" throughout the proceedings.

I made my closing argument at the end of a hard fought day. As persuasively as I could, I argued that the grandfather should have been able to see the cow. It was one of a herd of around twenty spread out along the road, and they were all Holsteins, with large white areas on them. The investigation showed the grandfather's bright lights had been on at the time of the accident. Police investigators can tell by looking at the burned out headlight filaments, and testimony from the accident investigation officer proved it.

Marlene was not at fault, I argued. She was facing bright headlights of the good Samaritan who stopped in the oncoming lane in an effort to be helpful. In her lane was a dark blue car stopped in the roadway without lights. The road was straight. How could she be at fault when the grandfather, with much better visibility ahead of him, bright lights on and no oncoming lights to blind him, had struck the cow?

The jury was dismissed for the evening, to begin deliberations the following day. I drove home in the dark, tired, but confident the jury would see things my way. About twenty miles south of the courthouse, for the only time in my life, I struck a deer.

I was trying a case somewhere in southern Iowa when a relative of one of the parties came into the courtroom to watch part of the proceedings. He was an older gentleman with a shock of white hair and wearing bib overalls. As he walked down the center aisle toward the public seating, like the good Catholic he no doubt was, he turned respectfully toward the judge...and genuflected.

Not long before I retired, a car wash was being proposed not far from our home, and a rezoning was necessary to build it. Several neighbors approached me about making a presentation at the rezoning appeal. I was happy to do it because I wasn't in favor of locating a car wash there, either.

On the evening of the hearing I worked late and just made it to city hall on time, bringing my briefcase full of work I planned to do at home. I picked up my wife, Janelle, to attend the hearing with me, to demonstrate family unity on this heated issue.

The city council chamber was filled with neighbors and others who lived near the proposed car wash property, all or nearly all vehemently opposed to the project.

City council meetings, usually staid and boring, sometimes yield to passionate feelings on all sides. Public hearings on zoning issues can become especially raucous and somewhat uncontrolled.

When it came my turn to speak, I pulled notes out of my brief-case and made my pitch to the council to deny the petition for re-zoning. Rising to a tempered climax of low-dose emotion and, I hoped, a reasoned argument, I thanked the council, turned on my heel, and strode out of the chamber to much cheering and applause. The perfect ending. Or so I thought.

We climbed into our car and I started the engine. The smile on my face evaporated when I realized I'd left my briefcase in the meeting at the lectern. I didn't dare go back to retrieve it, only to slink out again and ruin the moment. No, not me.

I sent Janelle in to fetch it.

Question: What's the difference between a trial lawyer and a new puppy?

Answer: With love, careful training, time, and endless patience, you can teach a puppy to stop whining.

(Told to me by a judge, and no, I don't think he was referring to me.)

Hello.

Hello, is this Mr. Jones, the lawyer?

Yes, yes it is.

Well, Mr. Jones, I understand you'll answer three questions for fifty dollars, is that right?

Yes, that's right. What's the third one?

A hunter visited a private hunting reserve at the same time every year. He always rented Lawyer, the best hunting dog the reserve had.

Lawyer could sniff out game, point, and retrieve better than any dog in the state. Energetic, dedicated and obedient, Lawyer was every hunter's dream. He commanded the highest fee of any dog in the hunting retreat's kennel.

One fall the hunter asked to rent Lawyer again and was told the fee would be only five dollars. "But last year the fee was a hundred dollars to rent Lawyer!" the puzzled hunter said. "Did he go blind? Lame? Lose his hearing? Or his sense of smell?"

"No," said the manager, "nothing like that. It's just that Lawyer was so good at his job we tried to think of a way to honor him for being such a great hunter. So we started calling him Judge. Now he just sits on his ass and barks."

(I told this to the same judge who told me the joke on lawyers and puppies, above.)

———

During my first year or two of practice I agreed to accept criminal appointments for representation of indigent defendants. The charges tended toward the mundane, but one case stands out.

A homeless man walking around downtown Davenport decided that a flower shop was an easy mark. It wasn't far from the bridge over the Mississippi, and rather isolated from other foot traffic. He walked back to his Salvation Army cot across the river into Illinois and hatched a plan. It was a simple plan. He would walk into the shop, terrorize one of the clerks, take all the money in the cash register, and get safely back into Illinois before anyone knew where he went.

To summon the necessary fear needed to motivate the clerk to quickly do his bidding, he needed a gun. He didn't have one. He asked his fellow guests at the Salvation Army if they knew where he could get a gun. No one did.

Maybe a knife would be enough. He tried to steal a butcher knife from the kitchen, but the knife drawers were locked. Undeterred, he somehow came into possession of a large firecracker.

Late one autumn afternoon he made his way across the Arsenal Bridge into Davenport and walked into the flower shop near closing time. He brandished the firecracker menacingly, and threatened to set it off unless the clerk gave him all the money in the till.

Soon he had the cash. Now for the getaway. With the money stuffed in his pockets and still carrying the firecracker, he walked back toward the bridge and was quickly arrested. Within an hour he was my client.

Plea negotiations seemed well justified. His pockets were stuffed with cash, the firecracker was in his jacket, and the flower shop clerk picked him out of a lineup. The lineup itself seemed rather unnecessary, but the prosecutor was especially zealous. In fact, he was out for blood.

My client was not just charged with aggravated robbery, but also the even more serious charge of assault with a deadly weapon. It was thought that the prosecutor was politically ambitious, and his behavior seemed to support this theory. A week later I had an animated discussion with him over coffee in the courthouse coffee shop.

JDS: Allan, I can understand the aggravated robbery charge. A firecracker can cause serious injury, that's for sure. But assault with a deadly weapon?

ALLAN: Even a rock can be a deadly weapon. So can a torch.

JDS: I agree. There are cases supporting those. But you can't show me a case where a firecracker was ever confirmed by a judge to be a deadly weapon.

ALLAN: There's always a first time. And the clerk might have had a heart attack. She was seventy-four years old.

JDS: Coulda, shoulda, woulda. She didn't. And she was pretty spry running out from behind the counter into the street to see where the perp went. And he didn't make any move to set it off. And he couldn't, which you well know. He didn't have any matches. You can't prove something that isn't true.

ALLAN: Doesn't matter. I don't have to show a gun has bullets in it. The victim has a right to assume it does. The flower shop clerk had a right to assume he had matches. He intended to terrorize her and he did.

JDS: It's not the same. You're right about the bullets, but a firecracker isn't a deadly weapon any way you cut it. Let's say he didn't have a firecracker and just lunged at her. Under your analysis, his body would be a deadly weapon because she could have a heart attack? You know you couldn't argue with a straight face that his body is a deadly weapon. The correct charge should be assault with intent to commit great bodily injury. Whether that charge is a winner or not is up to the jury. I doubt that it is, because you would have a very hard time proving intent. But a charge of assault with a deadly weapon won't wash.

ALLAN: File your motion.

I did. I filed a motion to dismiss the charge of assault with a deadly weapon and won. My client pleaded guilty to some lesser charge. The presiding judge seemed rather entertained by the events of the robbery and was perhaps more lenient than he might have been. I felt justice was done. More or less.

VIII
Collegiality

And do as adversaries do in law. Strive mightily, but eat and drink as friends.

-Shakespeare, The Taming of the Shrew, Act I Scene ii

Joe Martin was a genial lawyer who practiced for many years in Clinton, Iowa. He would often hoist a glass and exclaim, "God bless the man who sues my client!" What he was saying, in addition to giving thanks for the system that provided Joe and his family with their hard won bread and butter, was that lawyers owe each other the courtesy and respect that comes from trying to serve justice by serving opposing clients well.

Resentment, even hatred, of the opposition make for an unhappy life in the law and misses the point of the genius of our system of advocacy. Truth arises most dependably when opposing evidence, ideas, values, and interpretations of events clash in the courtroom under controlled conditions. And the job can be done with civility.

When conflicting stories and standpoints are tested with effective advocates before juries, justice is almost always done. But many lawyers take disputes too personally.

When I first started trying cases, it was customary for the opposing gladiators to retreat to a watering hole within walking distance of the courthouse and drink beer together until the bailiff called with the verdict. That tradition is long gone. Part of the reason, I think, is that trials take so much time that lawyers find themselves deep in accumulated work and head right back to the office to deal with it.

Another part of the reason is that lawyers don't get along as well as they used to. Backstabbing, sharp practices, tricks, and shenanigans can poison the atmosphere for social interaction and reasonable cooperation with our brethren.

A final reason, in my view, is that some plaintiff's lawyers have come to resent defense lawyers as standing between them and what they feel is their well-earned fee. Defense lawyers, on the other hand, sometimes view plaintiff's lawyers as unprincipled rascals willing to say or do anything for money. There's some truth in both viewpoints, but not universal truth by any stretch.

Joe and I were involved in an unusual case that lasted several years, but not quite as long as World War II. A non-profit civic organization called The Clinton County Development Group had attracted a huge petrochemical company called Chemplex to an outlying area of Clinton County.

The company refined petroleum feedstocks into low-density polyurethane pellets for industrial and commercial uses. The tiny white circles in Styrofoam cups, coolers, and insulation board are the end product of this process.

Chemplex agreed to locate in Clinton County, but only if the city of Clinton (the county seat) and the small neighboring town of Camanche agreed not to annex the plant for ten years. Chemplex felt that if city property taxes were levied during the start-up years, the enterprise might not reach profitable levels and would have to shut down.

As an inducement to Chemplex, and with the encouragement of the officially neutral Clinton County Development Group, the cities entered into an annexation moratorium agreement for an area of the county containing several square miles, including the proposed building site, for ten years.

The agreement contained two main parts. First, Clinton and Camanche agreed not to use their powers of involuntary annexation to bring the tax-rich property into their city for ten years. Second, and most important to our situation, voluntary annexations were permitted. In other words, if any property owner within the land covered by the agreement requested that their land be annexed, neither city was barred from accepting their land. Critically, however, the cities agreed not to *initiate or promote* voluntary annexation activities during the life of the agreement.

Chemplex subsequently built a sprawling refinery that can be seen for miles, rising out of the cornfields. High in the air, plumes of burning gas light the evening sky. During the ten-year treaty, a satellite plant, Hawkeye Chemical, was also built and incorporated into the moratorium agreement.

As the moratorium was just a few months from expiring, a number of farmers around the two plants began to worry. Their farms were within the land covered in the moratorium agreement. They did most of their business in Camanche, had their friendships and relatives there, and loathed the idea of being annexed into much larger Clinton along with the plant.

Clinton was much farther away and had an inferior reputation among the farmers, compared to Camanche. Many felt Clinton's municipal services were subpar, and property taxes were substantially higher than those in Camanche. The farmers' bottom line was, if they had to be annexed, they would much prefer to become residents and taxpayers of Camanche.

Several leaders among the farmers approached the Camanche town fathers about what to do. The town's attorney didn't know what to do, either. He persuaded the city council to hire our firm out of Davenport to advise them. Arthur Middleton, Sr., now recovered from his nearly fatal heart attack, assigned the novel problem to me.

In consulting the statutes, I learned that Iowa law required that part of the boundary of the land sought to be annexed to a municipality must be "contiguous," or touching, the border of the city seeking to annex it. In other words, a city couldn't leapfrog over some county land to annex a more valuable piece.

Neither Chemplex nor Hawkeye Chemical had a common boundary with Clinton. Several farms lay in between. Thus, Clinton would have to annex the farms along with the plants to provide contiguity, or a common boundary, with Clinton.

In examining the moratorium agreement, I confirmed there was no bar to voluntary annexations to either community by farmers adjacent to the plants. As long as at least one farm bordered the city limits and they all bordered each other, unlimited voluntary annexations were expressly permitted.

The farmers' concern was that unless something was done, the councils of both cities would pass resolutions of involuntary annexation almost simultaneously when the moratorium agreement expired. The principle of "first in time, first in right" would apply. But as 12:01 am rolled around and both councils passed resolutions, who could be sure which resolution of involuntary annexation was passed first? How could anyone tell which clock in which town hall was more accurate? What if the cities passed competing resolutions at exactly the same time?

These uncertainties and proof problems appeared impossible to sort out. We knew that settlement was equally impossible, and that Clinton had set its sights on annexing both plants.

I fashioned a rash strategy for presentation to the Camanche City Council. Statutes allow for governmental discussions involving land acquisition to be conducted in private. I recommended a resolution to go into closed session and presented a proposed draft to the council. They agreed, passed the resolution, and moved into the adjacent firehouse for further discussion.

Standing between the fire pumper and the snowplow, I laid out my plan and took questions from the council members. I suggested that while we couldn't "initiate or promote" voluntary annexations, we could legally advise the farmers wishing to be annexed that they could prepare voluntary petitions for annexation to Camanche. If every landowner in the disputed area submitted a valid petition for voluntary annexation, and if Camanche accepted the petitions, we would create an insulating doughnut around the petrochemical plants, preventing the common boundary Clinton needed to annex the agricultural land and Chemplex.

The state highway right of way ran past Chemplex. The state, of course, owned the right of way. I discovered that somehow that land was not included in the moratorium agreement. This meant that we could involuntarily annex the right of way at any time. Doing so would shut off a corridor to the plants through the fortress-like doughnut of farms that Clinton could annex to create a common boundary with the plants.

After acceptance of all voluntary annexation petitions from the adjacent farmers and involuntarily annexing the exempted highway right of way, Camanche would be in the driver's seat. The town could then annex both facilities as soon as the moratorium agreement expired.

I cautioned that to do otherwise was to risk a long and expensive battle with Clinton over the plants, and no one could predict the outcome with authority. We knew from the publicly available minutes of a Clinton city planning group that Clinton was anxious to annex both plants. A negotiated settlement was unlikely. I hastened to add that my recommendation would probably result in a lawsuit, too, but Camanche would have the stronger hand.

The hour was getting late. I noticed that the town attorney had fallen asleep during my presentation. Perhaps the drama of the moment was lost on him.

The Town Council agreed to my plan unanimously. That was the easy part.

I advised the farmers that they could submit petitions for voluntary annexation from themselves and their fellow farmers surrounding the plants. If we didn't receive petitions from all of them, a corridor of county land, like a bridge over a moat, would allow Clinton to annex Chemplex and Hawkeye Chemical. If we failed, Camanche would lose the tax revenue the plants promised, and the farmers would become residents of Clinton. Our firm couldn't draft proposed petitions, give legal advice, or help them in any way. It was all up to them.

Finally, the preparations must be conducted in absolute secrecy. If Clinton got wind of the farmers' actions, the city fathers would try hard to frustrate their plans.

The little band of farmers went forth to organize their neighbors. There were no lawyers in Camanche other than the town attorney, and he couldn't help because of the moratorium agreement. The farmers felt it was too risky to hire a Clinton lawyer. Word could get out.

On their own, the farmers leading the charge looked up the law to see what was required. They held organizational meetings at kitchen tables and called other neighbors they barely knew. They secured copies of tax maps and ownership records from the County Auditor and Recorder's offices.

Over the course of a few weeks, they managed to secure witnessed signatures on over twenty voluntary annexation petitions to the City of Camanche. Meanwhile, I prepared an involuntary annexation resolution for the state highway right of way.

The farmers presented their petitions with a flourish at a regular meeting of the city council. All were accepted by resolution. The council also passed the resolution of involuntary annexation I had prepared for the highway right of way running past Chemplex. If these annexations held up, Clinton would be prevented from annexing either plant, and only Camanche land would border these tax-rich properties when the moratorium agreement expired.

The headlines exploded. The *Clinton Herald* screamed that Clinton was being knifed in the back. I was branded a "land grabber." Relations between the two communities, never exactly warm, were as bad as ever.

I was deluged with phone calls from the media and from Clinton residents calling me every name they could imagine. As expected, Clinton sued.

Lengthy motions, discovery, and general pandemonium followed. The farmers' voluntary petitions were scrutinized for errors. Land records were scoured for defects in ownership of the farms. Depositions were taken of the farming couples who signed the petitions. My role was carefully examined for any hint that I had "initiated or promoted" any or all of the voluntary annexations.

There was no such evidence because it didn't happen. Every member of the farm families testified they were acting on their own, with no direction or help whatsoever, other than a two-minute conversation in which their leaders were advised of their rights under the moratorium agreement.

The moratorium agreement was a public document in both cities, meaning that what I told the farmers' leaders was nothing they couldn't have learned on their own. I hadn't "initiated" anything. The farmers came to us. I didn't "promote" anything. The farmers were already self-motivated to annex their farms and homes into Camanche.

There was a "David and Goliath" flavor to the battle. Several high-priced lawyers represented Clinton. Camanche had just me on their side. Chemplex had their own lawyers from Chicago enter the fray, siding with Clinton, even though Clinton's industrial tax rates were substantially higher than those in Camanche. I was treated like a pariah, with much invective and accusatory talk hurled in my direction.

Through all this, one of Clinton's team of lawyers, Joe Martin, was unfailingly courteous, kind, and professional toward a young, untested lawyer he barely knew. In spite of the circus atmosphere, name-calling, and white-hot tension, Joe was both a gentleman and highly effective in his representation of the City of Clinton. I now believe I subconsciously began to adopt his attitude toward opponents as my standard for professional conduct.

Joe died several years ago. I never had an opportunity to tell him how grateful I was for his courtesy, and how my professional life was affected by his example. I regret it still.

After much legal maneuvering and effort on both sides, the parties agreed to settle. Clinton agreed to annex Chemplex and would buy a tiny corridor of land from a willing farmer to make the plant boundary adjacent to the existing municipal boundary. Camanche agreed to annex Hawkeye Chemical but would not have to buy a corridor of land because a common boundary already existed. Other than the tiny corridor sold to Clinton, the farms voluntarily annexed would remain in Camanche.

The settlement reflected equity to both combatants. Clinton's municipal needs, much greater than those of Camanche, received a revenue stream from Chemplex proportionate to its size. Tiny Camanche received a smaller revenue stream from Hawkeye Chemical, but entirely proportionate to its municipal needs. A perfect settlement along the same lines could have come long before our legal services were necessary, but it was clear to all that relations between the two cities were so strained that talks before the moratorium agreement expired were highly unlikely.

IX
Shenanigans

The louder he spoke of his honor, the faster we counted our spoons.
-Ralph Waldo Emerson

I often tried cases in small county seat towns in central and eastern Iowa and western Illinois. Small rural counties present interesting challenges for the out of town lawyer. For one thing, the opposing local lawyer probably knows everyone on the jury panel. If he doesn't, his wife, cousin, dad, or ex-wife does. He knows many of the interrelationships among the candidates for the jury. He knows things I'll never find out in questioning the panel. He sits in church with several members of the pool of potential jurors. He knows the judge, his foibles, strengths and vulnerabilities. He does business with the hardware store owner who may turn out to be the jury foreman, a powerful and influential position.

In small communities everybody knows just about everybody. Jurors may well know others or even be related to others on the jury, for better or worse. Some may carry grudges of one sort or another and can be counted upon to disagree in deliberations or discount whatever the subject of the grudge says. Small town life for the out of town lawyer can be complicated. My Trial Practice professor, Bill Tucker, had an investigator take photos of the houses of all prospective jurors. He thought he gained important background information in that way. I never went that far.

I was assigned the defense of a routine traffic injury suit in the far corner of northeast Iowa in the mid-1990's. Depositions and other discovery went well over the course of a year or so leading to the trial date, and I rather enjoyed the company of the local lawyer representing the plaintiff and his wife. Jim Snyder, my opponent, was even tempered, friendly, and hospitable. He was gracious in offering phones, copy machines, and even the use of a vacant office for preparation work between depositions. There was always a big bowl of M&M's on his conference table.

Some lawyers ingratiate themselves with opposing counsel to try to create a *bonhomie* conducive to settlement when the opportunity presents itself. I tried to be attuned and sensitive to this behavior, while at the same time returning the courtesy as far as the adversarial relationship would permit. I felt Snyder's friendly attitude was genuine, and took a liking to him.

The lawsuit itself was somewhat sensitive because the claim was for a sum vastly in excess of the insured's policy limits. Ted Marks' insurance company engaged me to defend him up to the policy limits. But Ted had the right to retain his own attorney to represent his separate financial interests above the policy limit and to make demands upon his insurance company, through me, to settle at or below his limits to protect his personal assets if at all possible.

Ted chose not to retain separate counsel, which put me in the delicate but common position of representing Ted exclusively. Liability was clear. Ted had failed to yield the right of way. On the other hand, alleged injuries to Marvin Engelbrecht, the other driver, were questionable.

The first day of trial was easy enough. The judge proved competent and her rulings were sound. The jury was selected by mid-afternoon, and opening statements were concluded by both sides. My cordial opponent was his usual professional self and went out of his way to suggest a restaurant for my evening meal.

On the morning of the second day of trial I sensed Ted was uncomfortable. The trial was proceeding normally, with the usual ups and downs of witness testimony. All in all, I felt secure that Ted's personal assets weren't at risk and felt no pressure to settle.

In late afternoon the jury was dismissed and we reviewed the day's events. Ted seemed satisfied, but unhappy somehow. I asked if there was anything bothering him. Reluctantly, Ted confided that his sister-in-law was a secretary in Jim Snyder's law office. At the end of the previous day, Snyder had returned to the office crowing over his strategic successes during the day, and how I'd blundered in so many different ways he had a hard time recounting them. He marveled that my insurance company client had retained such an incompetent fool. Alarmed, Ted's sister-in-law called him with this news during the evening. She made Ted promise not to tell me, reasoning that her boss's confidentiality would be breached.

Now Ted was wondering if he'd made a mistake in electing not to retain his own attorney. We got along well, but now he had deep second thoughts about my legal ability, thanks to my opponent's unrestrained glee the previous afternoon. After all, Ted had no legal training and Jim was a respected lawyer in this small and pretty college town. Ted now had some reason to believe that his savings, his car, and even his home were at risk. Ordinary folks thrust into the courtroom are usually a bit frightened by the experience, but now Ted was really scared.

I briefly considered asking the judge for a postponement of the trial so Ted could secure a personal attorney. I felt the motion would prove futile, but worse, the judge might try to compel me to reveal the source of the information causing Ted to have a change of heart. I thought the chance was remote, but if it happened, Ted's sister-in-law could be out of a job.

I told Ted the postponement would surely last several months while his personal attorney became fully familiar with the case. I doubted the judge would grant our request. Ted agreed that we shouldn't ask for a postponement.

I had nothing else to offer. I assured Ted that to my knowledge I'd made no serious stumbles at all, and was reasonably sure the trial was going well.

As I often told clients in mid-trial, a basketball game can be as dramatic as a court contest. But it's different because the fans always know which team is ahead. The score is shown in big, bright, electrified numbers for all to see, and it changes after every score. Trials, not so much. Boxing matches and jury trials make for great suspense in movie dramas because during the battle nobody knows for sure who's winning.

I suggested to Ted that I didn't believe his assets were seriously at risk, and if I thought so, I had an obligation to recommend that the insurance company consider settling the case. I wouldn't make the recommendation because I didn't believe we had an unacceptable risk of losing. I told him I'd been trying cases much like his for many years, and I felt as confident as I could reasonably be at this point in the trial. Ted reluctantly agreed.

The third day went the way of the previous two, ebb and flow, ebb and flow. All in all, a good day. I explained every battlefield decision to Ted at the end of the day, and he seemed resigned to his fate, whatever it was. And the next morning Ted reported what his sister-in-law told him Snyder had said at the end of the previous day about my hopeless legal ability. Unfailingly professional and courteous during the day, Snyder turned into a laughing, sneering jackal in late afternoon at my expense and to the detriment of my relationship with Ted.

On the fourth day, Jim Snyder called Marvin's wife to the stand. She wasn't in the car when the accident happened, but she was both a plaintiff and a witness. In her plaintiff's role she was claiming damages for being required to care for her husband during his recuperation. She also claimed damages to her own enjoyment of life. She and Marv couldn't go bowling together or participate in other family activities while her husband was allegedly healing from the accident. In her witness's role she testified to the pain, suffering, and loss of freedom of movement her husband showed following the accident and continuing right up to the trial date.

I began a light cross-examination armed with a minor contradiction between the trial and deposition testimonies:

JDS: Mrs. Engelbrecht, you told us on direct that your husband used a cane for almost three months following the accident. Do you recall that?

WITNESS: Yes.

JDS: Do you recall being present when your husband, Marvin gave his deposition in Mr. Snyder's office last February?

WITNESS: Yes.

JDS: And you were present to hear all of my questions and all of your husband's answers?

WITNESS: Yes.

JDS: And Marvin was sworn to tell the truth in his deposition, correct?

WITNESS: Correct.

JDS: Beginning on Page 66 Line 12 of Marvin's deposition transcript your husband said, quote, Oh, I guess I was on that cane for about three weeks, a month after the wreck, unquote. Do you remember that?

WITNESS: No.

JDS: Your Honor, may I approach the witness?

The Court: You may.

JDS: Mrs. Engelbrecht, I've highlighted in yellow the testimony I just referred to. Here it is. I'd like you to read it to the jury if you will, please.

WITNESS: That's what it says.

JDS: No, please read it aloud.

(WITNESS COMPLIES)

JDS: Does that refresh your recollection that your husband was using a cane for less than half the nearly three months you just testified to under oath?

WITNESS: *I think I could remember better if I wasn't so nervous.*

Bells rang in my head. Mrs. Engelbrecht didn't appear nervous at all. More important, by the sheerest chance I'd heard that same answer before. I'd previewed a video at my office designed for plaintiff's lawyers who need help in preparing their clients and witnesses for court testimony. When a witness is cornered, the actress on the tape gives that same answer as a way out of the box, and generating some sympathy for the "nervous" witness to boot.

Our firm chose not to buy the tape because the suggested tips and techniques put words in the mouths of witnesses, and we didn't agree with that philosophy. I sensed an opportunity to put the lash to my opponent's back.

A lawyer should never ask a question unless he knows the answer in advance. Here, I didn't absolutely know the answer, but I had a strong hunch. I could bluff by my tone of voice. I learned early that if I dropped my voice at the end of a question, it would invite an admission I had reason to know was the truth. The goal now was to make Mrs. Engelbrecht the innocent victim and her lawyer the villain. Gently, I went on:

JDS: That's an interesting answer. Of course, Mr. Snyder has worked with you before today, telling you what to expect, hasn't he?

WITNESS: Yes.

JDS: You and Marvin and Mr. Snyder have spent many hours together, preparing for this moment, haven't you?

WITNESS: Yes, I guess.

JDS: And reminding you that you're under oath this afternoon, Mrs. Engelbrecht, Mr. Snyder told you to watch a video he provided to you, didn't he?

WITNESS: Yes.

JDS: And the videotape you watched told you how you were supposed to testify if you were caught in a misstatement, didn't it?

WITNESS: Yes.

JDS: And Mr. Snyder's videotape told you to say that you couldn't remember because you were so nervous, didn't it?

WITNESS: Yes.

JDS: And in fact, you performed for this jury with the very words the actress who performed on the video used, didn't you: quote, I think I could remember better if I wasn't so nervous, unquote?

WITNESS: Yes.

JDS: You aren't nervous, are you?

WITNESS: Not really.

JDS: But you did what Mr. Snyder's tape told you to do, didn't you? You claimed *under oath* that you were nervous as a handy excuse for your misstatement, correct?

WITNESS: Yes.

JDS: But it wasn't true, was it?

WITNESS: No.

Snyder perhaps could have objected on the grounds that I was invading the attorney-client privilege and a separate privilege called "attorney's work product." These privileges protect the conversations and preparations between attorney and client from disclosure. He either didn't know that or made a judgment call on the fly that he shouldn't object.

Ted sat up a little straighter in his chair. Attorney Snyder looked foolish and unethical, and we scored a few modest points for our side as well. I generally made it a practice to treat opposing counsel with respect, but Snyder had it coming, good and hard. And he never knew why.

Expecting an award in a small amount for the plaintiffs, I was especially delighted that the jury returned a verdict of zero dollars instead. So was Ted.

Jim Snyder and I crossed paths again, just once. The jury sent him home empty-handed the second time as well.

———————

In Engelbrecht vs. Marks I encountered some mild wrongdoing by my opponent and was able to expose it to the jury and take advantage of it. In Evans vs. Locust Street Shell I met a similar opportunity, but the ethical breach was more serious.

Fred Evans was an older gentleman, slightly built, with a special fondness for his big Ford LTD automobile. Fred liked a clean car, so he regularly bought gas at the Shell station in central Davenport, which offered a free car wash with a fill-up. One afternoon Fred topped off his tank and drove around to the rear of the station for his car wash, as he'd been doing for years. A prominent sign read,

HONK HORN
WAIT FOR ATTENDANT

As he always did, Fred honked his horn. The attendant didn't arrive. Fred waited. He honked again. Still no attendant came to press the button to start the wash.

Fred knew the routine. He knew where the button was. He drove up along the tire guides to a point where the mechanical hook would pull his car through the wash. He put the transmission in neutral and got out, walked over to the wall and pressed the button, setting the machinery in motion. He started back to his car to get in.

But Fred took too long. The hook caught the car underneath. The LTD lurched to life and began its lumbering journey through the wash. Fred ran the rest of the way to the car. He got the driver's door open and struggled to get into the moving vehicle. But a large, whirring mechanical brush pinned him between the door and the car frame, pulling him slowly through the spray and depositing him on the concrete floor on the other side of the brush.

Fred's LTD continued its trip through the wash and was pushed out the other side. The attendant saw it, dripping and unoccupied, with the door open. He ran into the wash and found Fred in a heap, soapy and soaking wet, but apparently uninjured.

The attendant helped Fred to his feet, took him into the office and tried to dry him off. Fred assured him that he was okay but a little shaken up. He was still angry that the attendant hadn't shown up to start the wash.

The attendant retrieved Fred's hat, put it on his head, and helped him into his car. Fred drove home without incident. He ate dinner, watched TV, and went to bed. Several hours into the night, Fred died of a heart attack. His widow sued the Shell station for wrongful death.

The law governing this case told me the facts were similar to the GPC grain auger trial I'd abjectly lost many years earlier. The plaintiff in that case exceeded the scope of his invitation on the premises by leaving his waiting area. He walked out onto the production floor, grabbed a push broom, and pushed gluten product into a floor-mounted screw auger to load his truck faster. He slipped on a loose grate, fell into the churning auger, and lost his entire left leg and a portion of his scrotum.

Similarly, Fred moved from a permitted area to a non-permitted area after losing patience with the unresponsive service station attendant and was swept into the car wash machinery as a consequence. The same legal principle applied in both cases.

The lesson I took from my crushing GPC defeat was that I'd be running the risk that a technical defense could be seen by the jury as hyper-technical, and resented when sympathy for the other side outweighs it. Although I had a technical trespass and perhaps even an "officious interloper" defense in this case, I chose not to use either. In the GPC suit I had introduced both, and lost a very large amount of my client's money.

In addition to arguing the station wasn't at fault, we contested the medical issue of whether the incident caused or contributed to the heart attack several hours later. It was an uphill climb. Physicians and lay people alike often implicitly accept the logic of, *post hoc, ergo propter hoc* (Latin meaning, "after the event, therefore because of the event").

Pretrial discovery was routine and uneventful. In response to our motion for production of documents we were furnished with a letter of opinion written by Fred's doctor to his widow's attorney supporting the claim that the car wash incident caused the delayed heart attack.

I proceeded to trial, prepared to lose on that issue. I concentrated our defense on the lack of negligence and the unforeseeability of this unusual event.

The trial proceeded predictably, without any major surprises. Fred's personal physician took the stand and testified consistent with his letter to Fred's lawyer containing his opinion that Fred's death was caused by the incident.

During his direct examination by Fred's lawyer the physician referred to his file to refresh his recollection, as permitted by the rules. However, when a witness does this, opposing counsel is entitled to review the physician's entire file for purposes of cross-examination.

Strictly on a fishing expedition, I asked for the doctor's file and a short recess to review it before cross-examining him. I thought there might be evidence in the file of previous heart attacks or maybe a history of heart problems that hadn't been disclosed in discovery.

My own heart rate quickened when I found a letter from the widow's attorney gently chiding the doctor for directing a "weak" report to the attorney addressing the cause of Fred's death. The lawyer went on to suggest substantially stronger language supporting the car wash incident as the cause of the heart attack. I noticed that the lawyer's suggested language was exactly what appeared in the report I was provided, word for word.

Digging further into the file, I found a copy of the doctor's earlier letter to the attorney stating the car wash event *could have* caused the heart attack. Under the rules of evidence, the doctor's first opinion wouldn't be medically certain enough to be admissible as support for the incident as the cause of death. Obediently, the doctor rewrote his letter using the lawyer's suggested stronger wording. The new letter read that the heart attack was indeed caused by the car wash incident, *within a reasonable degree of medical certainty.*

The trial resumed with cross-examination:

JDS: Doctor, you went to undergraduate and medical school for many years to become a physician, didn't you?

WITNESS: Yes.

JDS: And as you told us on direct examination, you took a written test over several days to demonstrate your knowledge and get you licensed to practice medicine in Iowa, correct?

WITNESS: Yes.

JDS: And you took an oral exam too, in which your examining doctors asked you to suggest diagnosis and treatment in a wide variety of situations?

WITNESS: Yes.

JDS: And you passed both tests?

WITNESS: Yes.

JDS: And in the course of your practice you've examined and treated many victims of heart attacks?

WITNESS: Yes.

JDS: Are you aware of whether Attorney Nichols ever went to medical school?

WITNESS: No.

JDS: Would you be surprised to know that he didn't?

WITNESS: No.

JDS: He doesn't have "doctor" in front of his name, does he?

WITNESS: No.

JDS: Your professional opinion in this case has changed, hasn't it?

WITNESS: I don't think so, no.

JDS: Well, during the recess I had your first letter to Mr. Nichols marked as Defendant's Exhibit 14. I hand you that exhibit now. Is this a part of your file?

WITNESS: Yes.

JDS: What is it?

WITNESS: You just said what it is.

JDS: (Laughs) What I say isn't evidence. What you say is evidence. Let's try again. What is Exhibit 14?

WITNESS: It's a file copy of a letter I wrote to Mr. Nichols.

JDS: At his request?

WITNESS: At his request.

JDS: And what's the date of that letter?

WITNESS: March 12, 1993.

JDS: Your Honor, the defense offers Exhibit 14.

Mr. NICHOLS: Objection. That's hearsay. No proper foundation.

JDS: It qualifies under the business records exception to the hearsay rule, Your Honor.

THE COURT: Sustained. Mr. Stonebraker, You have another chance. Can you lay a little more foundation?

JDS: Thank you, Your Honor. (Continuing) Doctor, you brought your office file to court today, to help you refresh your recollection, correct?

WITNESS: Correct.

JDS: And during your direct examination by Mr. Nichols you referred to your file for that purpose, right?

WITNESS: Yes.

JDS: And your file is kept in a safe and secure place in your place of business? Your medical offices?

WITNESS: Yes.

JDS: And you're the final custodian responsible for the security of your files, right?

WITNESS: Right.

JDS: Before an hour ago, was Defendant's Exhibit 14 contained in your office file on the deceased before I removed it for identification purposes?

WITNESS: Yes, sir.

JDS: We offer Defendant's Exhibit 14, Judge.

THE COURT: Any objection now, Mr. Nichols?

MR. NICHOLS: No objection.

THE COURT: Exhibit 14 is admitted.

JDS: And in that first letter you wrote that the car wash incident *could have* caused the heart attack, right?

WITNESS: Yes.

JDS: There's a lot of wiggle room in the term, *could have,* would you agree?

WITNESS: Sure.

JDS: The car wash incident possibly did and possibly didn't?

WITNESS: Yes.

JDS: That opinion doesn't rise to the level of what lawyers call *a reasonable medical certainty*, does it?

WITNESS: No, but I'm not a lawyer.

JDS: And you sent that letter to Mr. Nichols?

WITNESS: Yes.

JDS: And then you got a letter back from Mr. Nichols?

WITNESS: Yes.

JDS: Is this that letter?

WITNESS: Yes.

JDS: It's marked Exhibit 15?

WITNESS: Yes.

JDS: What's the date of that letter?

WITNESS: March 24, 1993.

JDS: And Exhibit 15 is a part of your file on Fred?

WITNESS: Yes.

JDS: And if I were to ask you all of the foundational questions the Court asked me to ask you on the admission of Exhibit 14, would your answers be the same?

WITNESS: Yes.

JDS: We offer Exhibit 15, Judge.

MR. NICHOLS: Objection, Your Honor. That letter is my work product and privileged.

THE COURT: Mr. Stonebraker?

JDS: First, Your Honor, I already have the letter. The work product privilege protects against disclosure, not the use of the material once disclosed. Second, Mr. Nichols knows that I am entitled to the entire file once the witness refers to it to refresh his recollection. Third, I have no other means of continuing with the subject matter of this cross examination without it. The letter clearly and sharply contradicts the witness's earlier testimony.

THE COURT: Overruled. Please continue.

JDS: Your first opinion wasn't good enough for Mr. Nichols, was it?

WITNESS: I don't know how to answer that.

JDS: Withdrawn.

JDS: (Continuing) So as soon as Mr. Nichols received your letter of opinion, he wrote back to you and told you it wasn't strong enough, didn't he?

WITNESS: That's what it says, yes.

JDS: He described your opinion as, "weak," right?

WITNESS: Yes.

JDS: And in fact, Mr. Nichols asks you to change your opinion, right?

WITNESS: Well, not really. He questions the wording of the first letter.

JDS: Well, the letter speaks for itself, but he specifically asks you to change quote, *could have caused*, unquote, to quote, *caused the heart attack within a reasonable degree of medical certainty*, didn't he?

WITNESS: Yes.

JDS: Mr. Nichols has no medical training to make that judgment, does he?

WITNESS: As far as I know.

JDS: No?

WITNESS: No.

JDS: So at Mr. Nichols' request, you changed your medical opinion, not for a *medical* reason, but for a *legal* reason didn't you?

WITNESS: Well, I clarified it.

JDS: Well, you changed it from quote *could have caused* to quote *did cause*?

WITNESS: Yes.

JDS And no medical fact or change in facts arose to change your opinion?

WITNESS: No.

JDS: Only Mr. Nichols' letter?

WITNESS: Yes.

Then I let this honest but naive physician off the hook, dropping my voice at the end of the question.

JDS: And in fairness to you, Doctor, you were anxious to be helpful to Fred's wife, the widow of your patient, in this lawsuit weren't you?

WITNESS: You could say that, yes.

The doctor was essentially an independent witness. I felt my opponent was guilty of witness tampering, or worse, encouraging perjury. Juries don't think much of lawyers in the first place. When one is caught manipulating the evidence, he's likely to walk away from the trial an unhappy man.

The doctor wasn't familiar with legal matters and, as strange as it sounds, I didn't feel he knew what he did was wrong. He was a general practitioner, and not wise to the ways of the courtroom as more frequent medical witnesses such as neurosurgeons, orthopedists, psychologists and psychiatrists are.

After a few years of trying cases I learned to tell with some sixth sense who was lying and who wasn't. Juries usually can as well. Whittaker Chambers described the phenomenon well in *Witness,* his superb account of the Alger Hiss Communist spy trials. Before the famous "Pumpkin Papers" were revealed, the case hinged on whether Chambers, the accuser, or Hiss, the accused, was believed:

If the mass of people can hear a man's voice, listen to what he has to say, and his way of saying it, they will, not invariably but as a rule, catch the ring of truth, and pretty unerringly sort out a sincere man from an impostor.

This wrongful death trial had suddenly moved from a potential six-figure claim to something much less. Shortly after the doctor stepped off the witness stand, the suit was settled for a tiny amount.

X

The Judiciary

Judge: Young lady, are you showing contempt for this court?
Mae West: Why, no, Your Honor, I'm trying my best to hide it.
-Miss West, on trial for obscenity, 1927

Lawyers enter a rough neighborhood when addressing judges and judging, and in thirty years of trial practice, I've developed a few opinions. Now that I'm retired going on thirteen years, I feel more free to express my views.

I'll address only the state judiciary. Federal judges are nominated to a lifetime appointment by the chief executive and confirmed by the Senate. The states, however, are free to choose their own means of populating their judgeships.

Lawyers have an ethical duty to uphold the dignity and respect of the judiciary, and I'm still a lawyer. I have always held, and maintain today, considerable respect for the judiciary as a whole. Still, no institution is immune from criticism. To ignore the facts would include me in a conspiracy of silence. My thoughts are intended to criticize constructively, not destructively. Let's start by looking at how judges are selected.

Most states select judges by electing them in districts where there's a vacancy or where a lawyer challenges the incumbent. The system discourages challenges, however, for a simple reason reminiscent of one of Aesop's Fables called, *"Who Will Bell the Cat?"* The story imagines a group of mice living in a comfortable residence, but threatened by the house cat. A couple of mice were caught by the stealthy cat. Something had to be done.

The mice got together and decided the only way to warn themselves of the cat sneaking up on them was to put a bell around its neck. No one volunteered for the risky duty. The cat caught and ate the mice, one by one.

In similar fashion, a practicing lawyer risks much when contesting an election against a sitting judge, understandably jealous of his power, rank and perquisites. If he loses, the judge, being human, may take revenge on the loser. Often, no one dares to mount a challenge. The uncontested incumbent is elected again and again.

While democracy works well in most cases, popular election isn't the best way to place black robes on lawyers and gavels in their hands. There are many reasons. First, the general public doesn't have much of an idea who would be the best person for the job. Most voters never see the inside of a courtroom, and even those who do are ill-equipped to compare the qualities of one candidate to another, or a challenger to the incumbent.

Moreover, campaigns for judicial office are never very enlightening. All candidates express their reverence for following the law. All proclaim their view that criminals should be punished, and spout airy generalities like fairness and honor. What could be less useful to voters than these bland and predictable platforms? How can one candidate be differentiated from another when they all say the same things? What's less democratic than an electorate bathed in ignorance?

Second, it's demeaning to require judges to enter the crass political arena every few years. Judicial dignity suffers in the process, and, by turns, respect for the rule of law may be weakened.

Third, judges elected for a term of years face the possibility that the voters will turn them out at the next election, making the decision to run for the bench a risky one. Although most elected judges enjoy the security of re-election until retirement, the possibility of defeat at the polls is a sobering prospect. A defeated judge who must resume law practice starts anew, with no clientele and the stigma of having been turned out of office. This uncertainty may discourage the best potential candidates from running at all.

Worse, the judge in a highly emotional and publicized case may have one eye on the views of the electorate and the other on his future. Judges must be above the winds of popular opinion and decide issues solely on the law as applied to the facts.

Fourth, judicial candidates running for election must raise money for their campaigns. Lawyers are almost always the biggest contributors. Lawyer's spouses sometimes appear on donor lists as the contributors, fooling no one.

Elaborate rules of ethics are required to dictate when a lawyer may contribute to a judicial campaign and when he may organize a fundraiser for a candidate. Even if the rules are scrupulously followed, it's only human nature for some judges to "remember" a lawyer's contribution toward his campaign and look more kindly on his arguments than might otherwise be the case, even subconsciously. Even the appearance of impropriety in these situations presents a conflict of interest for the court.

Should a lawyer put a bumper sticker on his car for a judicial candidate? Should he put a supportive sign in his yard? Should he send a letter to the editor backing one candidate over another? What if a judge asks him to be his fundraising chairman? What if he declines? What should he do if he has a matter pending before the judge and he's awaiting a ruling? What if a lawyer honestly feels the challenger would make a better judge and supports him? And he loses? These tough questions and other concerns have been confronted by a few states, and different ways of selecting judges have been adopted.

Iowa has a system in which the governor appoints all state judges at all levels, and lawyers participate directly in the process. It's not perfect, but the most distasteful aspects of retail politics are absent. Judges are appointed to a six-year term, but must retire at a certain age. A generous pension provides lifetime security. The Iowa Supreme Court administers the district court system and enforces judicial standards of ethics. The Supreme Court may remove a judge for reasons of health, mental incompetence, or ethical violations.

Democracy plays a part in the process by way of a check and balance on what the electorate might feel was a poor judicial choice by the governor. Voters have the opportunity to approve or disapprove sitting judges on the ballot every six years.

Similarly, the electorate may recall all state judges on all levels, even on the Iowa Supreme Court. In fact, in an unprecedented move, a well organized group motivated enough voters to recall three Iowa Supreme Court justices in November, 2010 as a direct result of a highly unpopular ruling declaring Iowa's law prohibiting gay marriage unconstitutional.

Here's how Iowa's process works. When a judicial vacancy occurs, the county bar associations of the district in which the vacancy exists notify the lawyers living in the district of the vacancy. Those interested in the position submit their names and qualifications to a panel of district lawyers appointed to evaluate the applicants. Interviews are conducted and backgrounds are evaluated. The top two candidates are submitted to the governor, who interviews them and appoints one to the vacancy.

His term may be renewed for successive six-year terms if the electorate votes to retain him. If not, his term expires and another judge is appointed in his place by the same process.

Iowa's non-partisan system works tolerably well for two reasons. First, only a notoriously bad judge will come to the attention of the public sufficient for a majority of the votes to be cast against him when his name comes up on the ballot for a renewal of his term. The voter is asked a simple question on the ballot: "Should Judge Earl T. Smith be retained for a six-year term? Yes or No" If a fair-minded voter has no opinion, he tends to vote yes. If a judge has come to the attention of the voter for some controversial ruling, he may vote no. Majority votes in the negative are rarities, and should be.

Judges don't campaign for re-confirmation. This spares the judiciary and the public the vapidity of campaign speeches and teas in the homes of fawning lawyers, and the waste of money political campaigns would generate. It prevents the germination of influence and corruption that can arise from lawyers pushing candidates by funding, fundraising, in-kind contributions, and other support. Rejection at the polls is rare, providing some sense of job security for the judge and encouraging a wider range of candidates to make themselves available for appointment.

Second, before each election, the lawyers in the state's judicial districts conduct a survey, or "plebiscite" among themselves addressing whether each incumbent judge up for re-confirmation should or shouldn't be retained. The plebiscite results are published in the newspapers as an aid to the voters. Thus, judges run not against another candidate, but on their own abilities, as interpreted by the lawyers who appear before the judges regularly. The unspoken presumption is that lawyers are better able than the public to evaluate the suitability of the incumbents for retention.

The theory that lawyers know best who should and shouldn't be retained is thought to sometimes have the opposite effect from what's intended. The public may suspect that lawyers' disapproval of a certain judge is a good sign. The voters theorize that the judge must be holding lawyers' feet to the fire, and the judge ought to be retained.

In fact, when unfavorable plebiscite results are published in the newspaper reporters often contact the unhappy judge for comment, knowing they'll get a story. Some judges have interpreted the results differently from the plebiscite's unwelcome message. They're quoted as saying the results really show that lawyers were angry because the judge would strictly enforce deadlines, punish criminals more severely than the criminal bar felt reasonable, and generally demagogue their candidacy to improve their chances for re-confirmation. This behavior seems to have kept more than one poorly qualified judge in office when their approval ratings among the local lawyers were below 50%.

Only a few Iowa judges have been turned out of office by this process. To my mind a few more probably should have. Still, in general, many more problems are avoided by Iowa's system, touchy ethical problems don't arise, and judges escape the indignity of campaigning for a position an often uninformed public decides with their ballots.

Despite Iowa's enlightened method of choosing them, the state's judges aren't paid nearly enough. Many lawyers earn vastly more than judges. Good lawyers can choose what they want to do and whom they want to represent. They can specialize in limited areas of the law. Iowa judges, at least, don't have these luxuries. They're limited in when and how long they can take a vacation. Judges must be careful, even circumspect, in their social connections. They shouldn't have lunch with a lawyer, or even attend a football game with one. Since every major business in his district is not infrequently embroiled in litigation of one kind or another, a judge shouldn't socialize with officers or directors of companies he may find in his courtroom at a later date. Of necessity, the bench is a lonely place.

In most Iowa districts, judges must sit on probate, domestic, civil, and criminal dockets, dealing with everything that comes through the courtroom doors. As a result of the job description and the pay, and with many notable exceptions, we often attract mediocrities to the bench. Doubling or even tripling the compensation of judges would attract better candidates.

Some respond by saying that major league baseball umpires don't earn salaries comparable to what the players they control earn, but their skills rise to the highest level regardless. The analogy is inapt for two reasons. As important as umpires are, they don't have a choice to become ballplayers or not. Their skills lie elsewhere. I never heard of a ballplayer retiring to become an umpire, or an umpire leaving his chest protector and whiskbroom behind to become a shortstop. Judges, on the other hand, are lawyers before they assume the bench. Few but the most selfless top flight practitioners are willing to take a huge pay cut to serve as the law's equivalent of umpires. Mediocrities, as defined by their track record of legal and financial success, are often anxious to assume the safe, secure, and prestigious mantle of judge.

Second, the free market controls what umpires earn, and they have a labor union to represent them. Judges have no union and no constituency. The free market is absent from the decisions that control their compensation. Judges have nothing other than the caprice of the legislators who set their salaries.

On a handful of occasions I became aware of highly unethical behavior. I once received a call from a well-known Illinois lawyer with whom I'd just reached a settlement agreement. We'd just settled our case for a bit less than the policy limit in a personal injury claim. He asked if he could change the amount of the settlement shown on the release papers to the full amount of the policy limit. Under the law at that time, he could then make a claim against his client's own auto insurance carrier for a type of excess benefits called under-insured motorist coverage.

He wasn't asking for more money from my client. A deal's a deal. He merely wanted to falsify the amount we settled for to defraud his client's insurance company and was bold enough to say so. Of course, I declined. The lawyer is now a sitting judge in western Illinois. Illinois elects its judges by popular vote.

I never had the urge to stand for judge. The pay was far too low, and the work looked like drudgery. In a similar context to the lawyer/judge pay disparity discussed earlier, I thought of judging as akin to umpiring. I viewed myself as something like an everyday ballplayer who sometimes struck out, but often would get on base somehow, or maybe even hit a home run. I enjoyed the hitting, base running, fielding, the applause and the recognition, and even tolerated the boo's as part of the job description. But it was the competition that got me up in the morning, looking forward to the day. Umpiring never had that appeal.

XI
Lawyering

The first thing we'll do, we'll kill all the lawyers!
-Wm. Shakespeare, Henry VI Part 2, Act IV Scene ii

Often heard as a *cri de coeur* by those frustrated with what they see as faults in our system of justice, Shakespeare's dramatic exhortation sent the opposite message. The words were spoken to an unruly mob by a character the Bard called Dick the Butcher, an anarchist helping Jack Cade stir up disorder and chaos in fifteenth century England as the houses of York and Lancaster vied for hegemony. Civil unrest furthered the Duke of York's cause.

Through Shakespeare's eyes, lawyers were the protectors of civilization, not the bane of it. Killing all the lawyers would be a first and powerful step toward driving a stake through the heart of the settled social order Dick the Butcher and Jack Cade swore to disrupt.

One of the most commonly misunderstood elements of our legal system is the contingent fee. Lawyers willing to work for a share of an injured person's compensation sacrifice their honor and raise doubts about their credibility when they advocate a case they may not truly believe in, goes the argument. Let's examine the contingent fee and, in doing so, reflect in some detail on the philosophy of our system of justice.

First, a contingent fee agreement keeps the lawyer honest. Why? Imagine what could happen when a lawyer knows a claim has no merit, but encourages the client by telling him he has a great case. Heartened by the promise of riches, the client pays the monthly bill from his lawyer. This goes on perhaps for years. The lawyer loses the case, as he expected, but has been paid handsomely anyway. He blames the judge, the jury, the opposing lawyer, and bad luck. The client goes home broke and disappointed. His lawyer buys a new boat.

Contingent fees aren't appropriate in domestic disputes, most business law contests and real estate matters, among others. In personal injury cases, they're clearly appropriate and even preferred from an ethical standpoint to avoid chicanery and deception that's extremely hard to detect and redress.

Contingent fees ensure that the lawyer believes, along with the client, that the case is just or he wouldn't invest his time and resources in handling it. He may be proven wrong, and if so, he pays a heavy price in lost time and the compensation he might have earned in more lucrative work. In other words, both the lawyer and the client assume the risk of losing. Better for the lawyer to lose time and the expectancy of a fee than the client losing both the case and substantial money, perhaps even his life savings.

Second, contingent fees level the playing field between those wealthy enough to engage lawyers and those without funds to access the courthouse. Thus, the contingent fee helps keep the blindfold on Justicia, the goddess of justice holding the scales weighing the merits of judicial conflict. The contingent fee underscores the time-honored principle of equal justice under law, by offering the keys to the courthouse to all. The rich and the poor are indeed equal in the eyes of the law, and the contingent fee aids that principle.

The best civil trial lawyers usually believe in their client's case, and it shows in their advocacy. Criminal cases are different, of course. The criminal justice system is founded on the democratic ideal that even the worst of us are entitled to a zealous defense. A criminal lawyer need not believe in the justice of his client's case, but must advocate the best interests of the defendant anyway to protect the integrity of the system.

When a criminal lawyer puts on a sham defense or "lays down" without vigorously cross examining witnesses or introducing credible evidence because he believes his client guilty, justice suffers, and society suffers. The lawyer is substituting himself for the judge and jury, which abuses the legal system.

The advent of DNA testing is a good example of this principle. Over 250 innocent convicts have been released to date because irrefutable DNA evidence, developed after trial because the technology wasn't available when the accused was convicted, has freed prisoners once proved guilty *beyond a reasonable doubt.* Poor lawyering undoubtedly put many of these innocent Americans in prison.

And what of the prison population wrongly convicted, but a blood or other body sample has been discarded or lost? And what about the great majority of prisoners who weren't lucky enough to have body samples at issue in their cases in the first place? Projecting a fraction of wrongly convicted defendants into the larger prison system in the same ratio to those who have been freed by DNA evidence is disquieting to many. But DNA may indirectly lead to needed reforms in our method of appointing counsel to indigents.

One badly needed reform was the guarantee of the right to counsel, in the person of one Clarence Earl Gideon. Gideon was a small time crook who spent many years behind bars on various convictions. He put his time to good use, becoming an effective jailhouse lawyer. He'd demanded that a lawyer be appointed to represent him in his last criminal trial, but his petition was denied.

Gideon defended himself and lost. He appealed on his own, and with some excellent pro bono help along the way, his case went before the United States Supreme Court. He won the right to appointed counsel at public expense, and for indigent criminal defendants coming after him.

In *Gideon vs. Wainwright* the Supreme Court ruled that Gideon was entitled to a lawyer at public expense. He revolutionized modern criminal justice for the better. But what the Supreme Court didn't count on was the manner in which court-appointed lawyers are compensated.

Government-mandated rates are far below what lawyers are able to earn in other work. Lawyers willing to accept criminal appointments are often low achievers without more lucrative clients. Thus, a mendicant class of lawyers populates many courthouses, begging bowls firmly in hand, until their next criminal appointment rousts them from the coffee shop and onto their swaybacked warhorse, only to plead their new client guilty some months later. With many outstanding exceptions, the quality of legal representation is often poor in court-appointed cases, resulting in greater potential for miscarriages of justice.

Prosecutors understand the needs and motivations of the appointed indigent criminal lawyer. Indeed, many were once appointed criminal counsel themselves, before retreating to the relative safety of a regular paycheck and government employee fringe benefits. Prosecutors will often charge a defendant with every felony and misdemeanor the facts will reasonably support. They know when plea bargain time rolls around they'll have a number of throwaway counts they can dismiss while clearing the way for a guilty plea to one or more of the most serious charges. The prosecutor looks good because he's secured a conviction, and the defendant's lawyer looks good because his efforts have resulted in dismissal of several counts.

Judges are willing participants in this process. They know that if most plea bargains aren't approved the criminal trial docket would be overwhelmed. No system of justice could survive without paring the docket through dispositions arrived at in plea bargaining. Thus, a rough equivalent of justice is reached by way of a marketplace in which the subjective needs of prosecutors, judges and appointed defense lawyers are met in the service of expediency and economy. And there's no realistic alternative.

Fortunately, the wide majority of accused persons are indeed guilty. But that doesn't absolve the criminal justice system of responsibility for providing a vigorous and effective lawyer to every defendant. If court-appointed counsel were paid more, the quality of representation would rise. Either we believe in equal justice under law, or we don't.

Some states have adopted public defender programs, funding an office of full-time lawyers to handle all criminal appointments. These programs are a step forward in providing adequate representation to the poor. But idealism infusing public defenders at the beginning of their careers may give way over the years to a jaded, routinized and rote system of representing indigents day in and day out, resulting in a lower quality of justice.

Finally, salaries and budgets of public defenders' offices are usually set by state or county government and funded with tax dollars. The demands of dealing with potholes, parks, sewers and other public works keep public defenders' salaries at the low end of government budgets. The better public defenders often move on to greener pastures after a few years, leaving newly minted and inexperienced lawyers to fill the vacuum.

Partly in response to the often sub-par representation afforded indigent criminal defendants, appellate courts have recognized grounds for appeal based on "ineffective assistance of counsel." Now a convicted person may bring an appeal with a new lawyer and be awarded a new trial, and presumably more effective appointed counsel, when the evidence shows his original lawyer was not up to the task, and the lawyer's inadequacy likely played a role in his conviction. The right to complain of inadequate counsel is not limited to indigents, of course, and retained lawyers are just as vulnerable to the charge as appointed counsel.

Law schools teach law to students using a vehicle called the Socratic method. That is, most professors don't lecture very much. They ask questions designed to explore the subject with students in an attempt to arrive at answers through the reasoning that derives from questioning one's way through a set of facts to arrive at a principle of law. Law schools do not emphasize "how to do it" courses like trial practice. Other than a one-semester course teaching the most superficial rudiments, I had no training in the finer art of trial work.

One reason is that trial technique is like jelly in a bowl. It can't be reduced to a scientific or mathematic determinism. If it could, all lawyers would try cases the same way. Instead, the system leaves it up to lawyers to find their own way to the best means of representing clients before the bar of justice. The marketplace has filled the vacuum by providing lawyers with post-graduate clinics and seminars designed to develop the trial skills lawyers need in court. The National Institute of Trial Advocacy (NITA) is perhaps the most prominent. Herbert Stern, Irving Younger, Gerry Spence and others have carved out niches in continuing legal education using some methods and techniques occasionally at odds with NITA's approach and with each other. The bottom line is that there's no single means of effectively representing clients in court. Some important areas are ignored altogether. One tool sadly lacking in the arsenal of some trial lawyers is a basic understanding of human nature.

Human nature happens, like products of digestion happen. Not always understanding this, some lawyers present their cases in ways that fight with human nature, rather than befriending it. An example is the lawyer who insists during jury selection and opening statement that jurors shouldn't make up their minds before hearing all the evidence. Indeed, that's the rule. Judges constantly remind juries to keep an open mind until the last gasp of closing arguments.

The defense lawyer presents his evidence after the plaintiff's lawyer or prosecutor. He might show the palm of his hand during jury selection, turn it over, and note how the other side is completely different. He urges prospective jurors to wait until they hear both sides before making up their minds. The jurors often make a solemn promise to do it.

It's a laudable but nearly impossible task. Of course, lawyers can't invite jurors to decide issues prematurely, and shouldn't. But the process begins anyway. It doesn't matter much what the judge says to the contrary, jurors start making up their minds almost immediately. They start sizing up the lawyers and their clients even before they're selected as jurors. They decide whom they like. They can often see through artifice, inauthenticity, and fawning appeals. A deeply cynical joke among lawyers goes like this: *The most important trait a trial lawyer can have is sincerity. If you can fake that, you've got it made.*

In the early days of western movies, the good guys were clean-shaven and always wore white hats. The bad guys wore black hats and had mustaches. It was easy to tell which was which. Figuratively, from the beginning of a trial, jurors begin to put white hats on one side and black hats on the other. They develop sympathies with lawyers as well as litigants. They slowly add sand to the scales of justice, tipping them ever so slightly as matters progress. They don't all see things the same way, of course, but movement off dead center is almost certain.

The slightest things can matter. A lawyer toying with a paper-clip, or slouching in his chair, or prone to annoying habits of speech can alienate jurors. Mature judgments on important things often have their beginnings in subjective, smaller judgments on unimportant things. As Judge Herbert Stern, a superb forensic educator once asked, "You're a party to a lawsuit. Which would you prefer? An edge on the law? An edge on the facts? Or Abraham Lincoln as your lawyer?" Good question. Good advice. Lincoln was one of the greatest lawyers of his day, representing some of the largest railroads in the country while maintaining a commoner's touch with the jury. Conducting ones self naturally before the jury, directly, and without personal quirks, fosters a favorable impression not just for the lawyer, but his client as well. Taking the earliest possible advantage of the persuasive aspects of human behavior is the secret sauce of effective advocacy.

Like most jurors, I'm an early decider too, and for silly reasons. It's just human nature. If I'm stuck in an airport watching a sporting event between two teams I don't care about, I can't stay impartial for more than a few minutes. I justify rooting for one team or the other based on some subjective consideration. The team I choose might be an underdog. I tend to like baseball players who wear their pants the old fashioned way, like leggings. Or maybe the best player is unable to play due to injury, so I root for his team. Or, maybe I'll prefer the cut of their uniforms. But consciously, albeit irrationally, I'll choose a side. And I'll usually stick to it.

Jurors, or at least many of them, behave the same way. And here's the important part: the longer they develop and maintain a bias, the harder it is to tell themselves they made a mistake.

Early judgments are not final, by any means, but once the process begins it becomes harder and harder for jurors to switch the color of the hats they put on the heads of the parties and their lawyers. The lawyer who understands something about human behavior uses it to his advantage, but always within the bounds of procedural and ethical rules.

The first chance for a lawyer to directly address the jury is the opening statement. Jurors have been put through endless and repetitive questions in jury selection, some making them uncomfortable at times. They've been herded in and out of unfamiliar rooms. They're told what to do. They're present in court because they've been ordered to be there, on pain of contempt of court, thus temporarily sacrificing their freedom under judicial duress.

Jurors have had to make arrangements for their kids, their dry cleaning to be picked up, their mother in law looked after, their job covered, and their meal plans. They've been made to wait for perhaps hours while lawyers argue preliminary motions in chambers or examine jury lists.

Jurors have figured out some of the arcane words and procedures lawyers use. They have some curiosity over what the case is all about and are eager to hear something about it. They're developing some impatience with the process. Some appreciate the give and take among the lawyers and find it mildly entertaining. Others hate it. They're eager to hear the evidence, decide a verdict, get it right and get it over with.

The opening statement is a matchless opportunity for the lawyer to begin the process of persuasion. But he often wastes it. He'll run through a commonly heard litany starting with,

Ladies and gentlemen of the jury, I'm Attorney So-and-so, and I represent my client, Joe Jones. Joe is seated over there at counsel table with me. My paralegal, Jill, is there as well along with my partner, Jim Holmes. Jim's the one with the brown tie on, and Joe has a red tie on.

Joe thanks you and I thank you for your patience with jury selection today. We know it's hard to sit and wait, and to answer all the repetitive questions lawyers ask. I think I speak for Mr. Stonebraker as well as myself, we wish there was an easier way to do it, but I think the process works the way it's supposed to, and we're both satisfied that we have a fair and impartial jury.

Now, what I say is not evidence. What is evidence comes from the witness stand and from exhibits brought to your attention during the course of the trial. Judge Henderson will tell you, and I tell you now, that you must keep an open mind until you've heard both sides of the story.

If I or Mr. Stonebraker think a question is wrong or an exhibit shouldn't be put in evidence, we each have a duty to object, and the judge will decide who's right. But don't hold it against my client if the judge rules against me, or Mr. Stonebraker's client, for that matter, blah, blah, blah...."

By this time the lawyer has almost lost them. Instead, he should open with a punchy, clear statement of what the case is about, introducing his strongest points and also his weakest points. The ears of the jury are tuned to their highest level of attention. The moment shouldn't be squandered on pointless preliminaries. Better instead to begin with something like this:

On January tenth at around 8:30 at night three years ago, Mary Pringle was tucking her kids into bed, and getting ready to go to work at the county hospital in Mason City. At about the same time, George Kinsley was having his last glass of beer at the Oasis bar downtown.

By 9:30 pm Mr. Kinsley was working his way through a pitcher of beer at The Juke Joint out by the hospital, watching a basketball game on TV. About then, Mary started driving the fifty-one mile distance from her home near Plainfield toward the hospital to be on time to put on her nurse's uniform and prepare for the evening's patient care.

According to the register receipt, Mary paid for gas and a cup of coffee at the 7-11 at 10:19, about twelve miles from the hospital. By that time Mr. Kinsley was almost finished with his third pitcher of beer.

On his way to another tavern, and only seven blocks from the hospital, the intoxicated Mr. Kinsley crossed the center line of Highway 65 at 10:34 pm and struck Mary's minivan head on, killing her instantly.

The evidence will show exactly what I just told you. It will also show that Mary, in a sudden and desperate attempt to avoid the wreck, crossed the centerline to get out of Kinsley's way. Kinsley suddenly veered back to his own lane, where the head-on impact happened at a combined speed of almost one hundred miles per hour, and where Mary died....

This beginning grabs the jury's attention. Now they want to learn more. How old are Mary's kids? How are they doing? How much did she earn as a nurse? Was she struggling as a single mom, or did she have a husband? The lawyer can and should answer these questions and others in the opening, holding nothing back for later.

Opening statements are often called opening arguments. This is a misnomer. A lawyer may not argue during his opening, but he may set out the evidence he knows he can prove, and he may do so persuasively. If he does, he can begin to persuade the jury without argument.

The difference between statements and arguments is reasoning. If a lawyer applies reason to facts, he's arguing, and an objection by his opponent will be sustained.

When jurors start making up their minds, it's hard for them to change. They'll think, "Well, I'll wait until I hear all the evidence, like I'm supposed to." But they'll often entertain one side's presentation through an overlay of skepticism and perhaps an inhospitable attitude.

Most lawyers will tell you closing arguments are the most important part of a trial. They're wrong. Indeed, closing arguments are the last chance to persuade jurors, but many are already persuaded. The rest are leaning one way or the other. No matter how many times the judge admonishes jurors to keep an open mind, the dawn of persuasion begins the moment the bailiff opens court, and even before. It's well along at lawyers' final arguments.

Local lawyers often gather in courtrooms to listen to closing arguments. They're showing up at the wrong end of the trial. The real fulcrum of decision-making in most cases, absent some surprise that changes the course of events, is opening statements. I'll grant they aren't as firey or dramatic as closing arguments, but they're usually more consequential to the verdict.

Closing arguments should use logic and common sense to highlight the strengths of the case and minimize the weaknesses. Few juries are unanimous in their views of a case as closing arguments begin. The effective lawyer will arrange his argument to give the tools of sound reasoning to his friends on the jury, so they may use those tools to persuade his opponents during deliberations. A lawyer can't pull his own wagon in the jury room. He's not there. Jurors he's persuaded throughout the trial will pull it for him.

He doesn't know for sure who his friends are, but he has a hunch. Body language, smiles, scowls, note taking when he makes an important point, are all keys to both sides as the trial proceeds. He meets the eyes of all jurors during his argument, but he may fix upon a particular juror when making a point he has reason to believe that juror thinks is important.

He doesn't read his argument. He puts his notes, if any, on his counsel table. He takes a moment to consult his notes when transitioning from one major point to another, but he's willing to live with forgetting to make a point he's written down in favor of the vastly more persuasive power and energy of a spontaneous presentation.

Complex cases demand careful organization of closing arguments. One of my favorite means of organization was an analogy I offered when a theme was necessary to keep the attention of the jury, entertain them in small ways, and provide a basis for the deliberations they were about to begin. Like a preacher recycling his best sermons for different flocks, I used the analogy several times over. The theme was mustard seeds.

Ladies and Gentlemen, I'm going to talk about who is at fault in this case and who isn't. And then I'm going to talk about money. But first I'm going to talk about mustard seeds. In a few minutes you'll understand why.

In the fifteenth and sixteenth centuries, Spanish explorers started in Mexico and what's now Florida and spanned much of North America. They ranged far and wide in a search for gold. They found some, but mostly their efforts came up dry. They brought along large bags of mustard seed from Spain. Mustard seeds are very small, light, and store well. Bags full of mustard seed can be carried long distances on horseback.

One of the biggest challenges early explorers had was getting back to where they started. Going out on the exploration was easy. They roamed far and wide. Getting back was the hard part. They had to find a tiny spot on the globe where their ship would be waiting.

Unlike charting a straight course on the high seas, the course of an exploration on land bent and curved around mountains and hills, up rivers to fording spots, and down valleys conforming to the lay of the land. The Spaniards sowed mustard seed at turning points along the way. A rider on one of the first horses in the party would scatter the seeds. The following horses would drive the seed into the ground with their hooves.

Mustard flourishes in most soils, is drought resistant, and grows with distinctive yellow blooms. When the exploration was finished, explorers could find their way back to their ship over perhaps thousands of miles and years later, by following the mustard growth. They found their way back to where they started. And in this discussion I'm going to point out waypoints, like the Spanish used mustard flowers, to help you navigate through the evidence to your verdict.

The territory the jury will explore is as unfamiliar and foreign, in some ways, as the North American continent was to the Spaniards. A vast, daunting array of contested facts, human behavior, technical evidence, and unfamiliar legal rules and terms will confront them. They've been on a long and unfamiliar journey through the trial, and now it's time to go back through the trail of evidence to the whole point of the trip–a fair verdict.

In fact-intensive cases, I'd work through the evidence and liken the array of information points important to their verdict, one by one, as mustard blooms, some large and some small, helping the jury find their way through the wilderness of evidence to their destination. The analogy helped me both as a theme and as an organizing principle, and my juries as well.

In cases where my opponent argued his case by dazzling the jury with his footwork, my analogy, not original with me, was the octopus.

The octopus is a smart and amazing animal. He's soft and squishy and he must taste good. So all his life he manufactures a black liquid inky substance without knowing exactly what he's doing or why he's doing it. And he saves it against the day when he'll squirt a big dose of ink toward the face of some sea creature trying to eat him. In the murky darkness and confusion, the octopus escapes to live another day. And he'll make more ink and use it when he needs it to hide himself and get away again.

When my opponent would invite the jury's attention to an irrelevant matter, draw a wrong conclusion or attack me or my case without a basis, I'd trot out the octopus. Each one of a string of false premises or conclusions would be labeled, "more ink" and I'd explain why. Rinse and repeat. Sometimes jurors would giggle or smile every time I said, "Here's more ink." The goal was low-key entertainment laced with a lesson.

Mild entertainment in closing argument is important but risky. Showmanship shows, and can easily be overdone. The story must feel natural to the case, and must have a point that prompts jurors to nod in agreement. Some catastrophic cases don't lend themselves to its use at all, but when it's appropriate, entertaining stories illustrating a point can be critical to winning.

The entertainment aspect of an argument is not helpful because it's an attention-*getting* device, but rather, as an attention-*keeping* device. Long arguments bleed attention as surely as blood drains from an open wound. Analogies in closing arguments and sermons alike can serve the twin goals of holding the listener's attention and adding persuasiveness. Every preacher knows this. Not all lawyers do.

XII
Strife

The credit belongs to the man in the arena, who strives valiantly and comes short again and again, who knows the great enthusiasms, the great devotions, and spends himself in a worthy cause, who at best knows the triumph of high achievement and who, at the worst, if he fails, at least fails while daring greatly, so that his place shall never be with those cold and timid souls who know neither victory nor defeat.
                    -Theodore Roosevelt

Over the course of thirty years I tried between nine and thirteen jury cases each year. Some trials lasted as little as two days, while others lasted many weeks.

By the time trial arrived I tried to be sure I knew more about the case than my opponent, the judge, the witnesses, and the client. Preparation for every known contingency creates the opposing emotions of security that you've thought of everything and adjusted for it, and the terrible sense of insecurity that you may have missed something.

On the morning of trial I was always a little nervous, but it was a nervousness of anticipation—the nervousness of wanting to get on with it. Once jury selection started, everything was fine.

Some good lawyers I knew hummed a favorite song in their head to relax before trial began. One hummed the theme from the movie, *Rocky*. Another hummed, *Peaceful Easy Feeling* by The Eagles. I hummed, *You Are The New Day* as sung by The King's Singers. Decades later, athletes are often seen with Ipod and smart phone buds in their ears as they approach their contest. There's something about music that calms and emboldens competitors, at least a little. Still, I fretted over every variable I couldn't control. What if Witness X doesn't show up? How do I fill that block of time? What if Witness Y takes more than the two hours I've allowed for her? What if I'm unable to admit Exhibit T-29 into evidence? What if Witness Z changes his story?

These and a hundred other questions gnaw at the lawyer throughout the trial, and especially at night, when sleep is precious but fleeting. A bedside notepad is essential as last minute ideas and worries demand attention. Many notes seem ridiculous in the morning, while others make sense.

Sometimes even the most thorough preparation can't affect events. A hotly disputed trial in Iowa City provides a good example.

Iowa City is known as a liberal venue favoring plaintiffs, owing to two considerations. First, the large state university there harbors a liberal faculty that's the envy of Berkeley and Columbia. A brilliant professor on the jury can end up as foreman, and steer a verdict where he wishes.

Second, an outrageous verdict handed down in the mid-1980's gave many defense lawyers wobbly knees. A small church van transporting nuns rear-ended an eighteen-wheel semitrailer at low speed, resulting in little damage to the van and no damage to the truck. The semi driver sued the Catholic diocese for neck injuries, and somehow won a verdict of over $600,000. Some defendants' lawyers feared trying cases in Iowa City for these reasons. I and others, being less sure of an inherent plaintiffs' bias in Johnson County, defended many cases successfully there.

I did encounter some professorial types on jury panels in Johnson County, but found that more conservative rural residents and townsfolk easily outnumbered the wildly liberal academics. I found I usually had enough peremptory strikes and challenges for cause to eliminate or reduce to a small minority the academics I felt were book-wise, but often lacking in street smarts. I still describe Iowa City as a beautiful little Midwestern university town surrounded by reality.

Brain damage is among the most sensitive claims of traumatic injury a defense lawyer can face. The public rightly fears loss of brain function in themselves, perhaps even more than fear of cancer and heart attack.

Minor brain damage is in vogue among plaintiffs' lawyers because the diagnostic criteria are rather flexible and easy to advocate. Give a jury some evidence of a slight concussion, loss of consciousness for a minute or two, throw in claims of subsequent memory loss, confusion, and seemingly insignificant thought compromise, and millions of dollars in damages are in play.

Christine Chapman was a young, single Iowa City resident who had tried college and dropped out. She lived above her means, working in a university cafeteria to support herself and her black Toyota 4-Runner. She survived a single vehicle wreck in rural Johnson County when her previous 4-Runner rolled over several times and landed upside-down in a ditch, a total loss. Miss Chapman crawled out a window, called police and was taken to the hospital where she was treated and released.

Two years later she was driving her replacement 4-Runner in a nearby town when Stan and Gina Givens missed a red light and drove into the intersection at about thirty miles per hour. The smaller Givens auto clipped the 4-Runner in the rear bumper area, spinning Chapman around 180 degrees. Miss Chapman was again taken to the hospital, where she was treated for minor injuries and released.

She later claimed she'd lost consciousness briefly, but that didn't appear on any accident report or hospital record. She hired a lawyer and brought suit, claiming brain damage and an unspecified amount of money damages.

One of my partners was assigned the defense, and asked me to take "first chair" in the trial. He was concerned because his case had two explosive elements: first, minor brain damage claims have a high level of jury appeal. Second, the venue was ultra-liberal Iowa City.

I was reluctant to help. Only a few weeks remained before trial, and I felt there wasn't enough time on my schedule to master the case.

I looked over the file. Discovery was worked up well. Expert neurologists, neuropsychologists, economists, an accident reconstructionist and other witnesses were ready on both sides. Meanwhile, a case I had scheduled to try in the interim was delayed. I agreed to take the lead on my partner's case.

Minor brain damage can be characterized as similar to *dementia pugilistica,* or the "punch drunk" brain damage known to be characteristic of some veteran boxers and occasionally, pilots who have taken off and landed too many times on aircraft carriers. Pilots repetitively jerking their heads and necks back and forth due to the sudden, rapid acceleration and deceleration attendant to such forces can cause mental impairment over time.

Minor brain damage allegedly caused by an automobile accident is different. Unlike a single auto accident trauma, *dementia pugilistica* requires a great many minor traumas to the brain before it's diagnosed. Automobile accident lawyers depend on claims of loss of consciousness to invite a diagnosis of concussion, which, if linked to behavioral markers, can lead to a diagnosis of a type of minor brain damage that behaves similar to being "punch drunk."

My partner told me that Miss Chapman didn't seem punch drunk at all. She performed well in her deposition, looking at the examiner directly with her doe eyes, exuding sincerity. She was able to recall events and responded to questions normally. She earnestly explained her failure to report her claim of a brief loss of consciousness. She said she was confused by all the hospital personnel attending her and wasn't sure who the emergency room physician was. She was in a haze she described as "a blurry feeling."

Her expert witnesses had a full medical explanation for her behavior, of course, contradicted by our experts. Chapman had performed below the norms on her expert's evaluation testing. On the other hand, our neuropsychologist felt she was intentionally "dumbing down" on the battery of tests he administered. His results showed much more "scatter," or variability, than did Chapman's expert's results.

Our expert couldn't testify to his opinion that Christine was malingering, but the wide disparity between his test results and those of her treating experts cast doubt on her claims. I knew we had a battle on our hands, and a verdict of six or seven figures could be on the line.

Several days of trial went well for us. At the end of the first week Chapman's flamboyant lawyer called her work supervisor at the cafeteria. We assumed she'd be a typical "before and after" witness, testifying that the plaintiff was a good and careful worker before the accident, but had become forgetful, depressed, and inefficient afterwards. We'd been given a summary of the supervisor's expected testimony in discovery, and, feeling she'd have limited value as a witness, my partner had chosen not to depose her. I prepared no advance cross-examination.

Instead, the supervisor laid into Chapman on Christine's own lawyer's direct examination. Chapman was described as an undependable, unreliable, and untruthful worker both before and after the accident, thoroughly discrediting Chapman's claim. Chapman's lawyer tried everything in an effort to rehabilitate his witness. She wouldn't budge.

It couldn't get any better than that. We waived cross.

The supervisor's surprising testimony knocked Chapman's lawyer off balance, and it showed in his behavior over the next couple of days. His presentation seemed lackluster and a bit careless, as though he was just going through the motions. Hadn't he interviewed the supervisor? Had the supervisor misled him into thinking her testimony would be favorable? She presented as candid, direct and very credible. We sat back in wonderment, elated.

What could go wrong? Our evidence wasn't even introduced yet. The plaintiff herself hadn't testified. Chris Chapman's story would be colored by the jury's memory of her cafeteria supervisor's rebuke.

Our courtroom was unusual and ill-suited to jury trials. It's long and narrow, little wider than a pair of bowling alleys, but not as long. The judge sits at one end, public seating is at the other end, and the jury is arrayed along one side. The opposing lawyers and clients are seated together at one large table in the middle. One side's backs are up against a wall and facing the jury. The other side's backs are toward the jury. While the latter can turn ninety degrees toward the witness stand, the seating position is poor, and they can't directly observe the jury.

Although maneuvering space was awkward, I was glad we were assigned this courtroom. For one thing, I always arrived for the first day of trial so early I often preceded the custodian or whoever opened the courthouse for the day. I arrived early so I could choose the seats that gave me the best angle and proximity to the jury.

The other side would have to face the wall. By custom, once a position is established at counsel table the parties and lawyers tend to remain in the same seats for the entire trial.

A second reason I liked this courtroom was its cramped size. Designed more for trials to the court, a jury box was added when jury trials became more common many years ago, allowing even less elbow room. By contrast, the majestic main courtroom, with oil portraits of judges long forgotten, a high ceiling, beautiful woodwork and spacious counsel tables, may cause jurors to subconsciously think, *big courtroom, big case.* Conversely, our quarters would perhaps give jurors the opposite impression. At least, so I hoped.

In such close quarters it's not unusual for the lawyers and parties on both sides to talk among themselves at our common table during recesses, and an odd, strained camaraderie can develop. It was during one of these breaks with the judge and jury out of the room that I spilled a cup of coffee and thoughtlessly quipped, "Sorry, I must have brain damage." Christine and her lawyer laughed politely, and nothing more was said.

The next day, Chapman was called to the stand. We knew she'd be the last witness on her side, and were poised to call our first witnesses. After hearing about her condition from doctors, psychologists, an economist, and her friends for days, both we and the jury were eager to hear from Christine herself, and a crescendo of drama grew. Chapman fumbled, forgot, looked at the ceiling and generally behaved as though she was brain damaged. Unlike the genuineness and sincerity my partner remembered, she seemed about as sincere as the plastic flowers the cemeteries put out.

Wrapping up after an hour or so, her lawyer began a new line of questioning:

MR THOMAS: Christine, you've testified about the embarrassment your brain injury has caused you in social settings in the past, is that right?

WITNESS: Yes, sir.

MR. THOMAS: Have you had any similar, recent experiences that you can describe to the jury?

WITNESS: Yes, I have.

MR. THOMAS: Tell the jury what you saw and heard.

WITNESS: Well, yesterday during the afternoon break period, the judge and the bailiff and everybody were gone. Mr. Stonebraker spilled his coffee at our table.

MR. THOMAS: What happened then?

WITNESS: He said he must have brain damage.

MR. THOMAS: How did that make you feel?

WITNESS: Humiliated. Embarrassed.

MR. THOMAS: Anything else?

WITNESS: Well, two days ago we were in the hallway, all alone, and he spoke to me.

MR. THOMAS: What did he say? (*At this point I could have objected to the hearsay, but I sat, transfixed, listening to what I knew was perjury. Worse, I was afraid that if an objection were sustained, the jury would conclude I was trying to cover up something.*)

WITNESS: He teased me about being brain damaged. He said I was retarded.

MR. THOMAS: How did that make you feel?

WITNESS: Very depressed. Sad. I know I'll never be the same as before.

Christine Chapman had just accomplished a neat trick. She combined something that was true with something that wasn't true. She knew I couldn't truthfully deny the coffee incident, even if I wanted to, because there were witnesses present. My denial of the untruthful hallway incident would sound hollow. She and her lawyer knew their case was failing, and to turn it around they needed something dramatic. Their goal was to create anger, turning the jury against the opposing lawyer, throwing the momentum to their side and polluting our entire defense.

I was stunned. Nothing like that had ever happened before. I leaned over to my partner and whispered, "*Tell me again why I took this case?*"

As Chapman began to testify about my fictitious conversation with her in the hall, I thanked my lucky stars I had the side of the table facing the jury. It's natural for jurors to glance at the lawyers to gauge their reactions to dramatic testimony. Lawyers, of course, can't speak to the jury directly except during opening statement and closing argument. I found years before, however, that I could communicate with my eyes.

As Chapman began to attack me I tried to make eye contact with as many jurors as I could, with a bland but open expression. I moved my eyes from one juror to the next, and with my eye contact, I was saying, *"Are you buying this? Is this credible? Do you trust what you're hearing?"*

I chose not to challenge her fabrications in cross-examination. I wasn't sure I was capable of winging it, for one thing. Since I was now a character in the drama I didn't know if I could pull it off. And at best, I thought, the issue would turn into a, "He said, she said" tie. I stuck to the primary points she made about the physics of the accident and her injuries, reasoning that I could call her later as an adverse witness in our side of the trial if we chose to.

Attorney Thomas rested his case, and it was our turn. Taking advantage of an hour's recess, we rushed to the courthouse law library to see what could be done. We had witnesses lined up for the rest of the day, but we had to counter this powerful testimony right away, before it could sink in.

Lawyers can't testify, or "vouch" on behalf of their client. They may not testify for any purpose. That would be a blurring of roles and is strictly forbidden. We found an exception, however. In rare instances in which, through the opposing party's actions the lawyer becomes a relevant issue, the presiding judge has discretion to allow the testimony of a lawyer who has been personally injected into the issues.

Following the usual housekeeping motions after the plaintiff rested her case, we asked the judge for a few extra minutes in his chambers before beginning our presentation of evidence. I began by addressing the judge with what lawyers call a "professional statement." As officers of the court, lawyers may recite facts for the benefit of the judge, and recorded by the court reporter verbatim as part of the official record of the trial.

Professional statements are not made under oath, and the lawyer is not subject to cross-examination. But a lawyer who speaks falsely before a judge is subject to severe punishment if he's caught. I told the judge what really happened.

Attorney Thomas had no reply. He had no research to offer. His argument consisted of the idea that anyone who had violated the rules of ethics by speaking to his client alone, and who embarrassed his client when he spilled his coffee should not be allowed to rehabilitate himself by addressing the jury with still more mischief.

Judge Vernon Ross listened to my professional statement and the arguments, examined the case law, and ruled I could testify. Fortunately, my partner was in trial with me, or I would've been sunk. I couldn't very well question myself.

I sat forward in the witness chair, unaccustomed to the reversal of roles. I was sworn to tell the truth. I never imagined I would ever be defending myself, and now, suddenly, I was. I tried to appear comfortable and confident, but serious and anxious to address this slur. My partner's questions allowed me to narrate as much as possible. Carefully, I explained the coffee incident in the context of the moment, and my lame attempt to cover my clumsiness with a self-deprecating but thoughtless remark. And then, the tables abruptly turned.

As I continued my testimony, opposing counsel stared at the wall behind my partner, rocking in his chair with his back to the jury, probably wondering why he elected to go down this road. Why? For this reason: I was now able to introduce something lawyers are almost never allowed to do. Because my opinion now had relevance to my testimony, I was able to offer my *personal* conviction that Miss Chapman had no brain damage at all. If I thought she really had brain damage when I spilled my coffee, I wouldn't have dreamed of mentioning it.

I noted that she'd told the story accurately, as far as she went. Her attorney and my co-counsel were also present. Although not exactly belly laughs, both she and her attorney laughed politely after I made the comment.

Equally important was what was not said. Her attorney didn't respond, "How dare you?" or, "How rude!" or, "That's highly unprofessional and we demand an apology!" or anything at all. I made a poorly chosen joke. They responded with mild chuckles, and that was that.

Addressing the supposed hallway remark, I testified that Chapman and I were never together in the hallway alone. And even if we had been, lawyers' rules of conduct strictly prohibited me from uttering anything at all to an opposing party outside her lawyer's presence. I noted that Judge Ross's frequent instruction to the jury not to talk to the lawyers during breaks applied to the lawyers and opposing parties as well. I had not violated that order.

Attorney Thomas had no cross-examination. I couldn't know whether the jury accepted my self-defense or not. It was time to go on. We presented our defense without incident over the next three days.

Closing arguments were a bit unusual. Christine's counsel brought into court an old-fashioned wind-up alarm clock with bells on top. He told the jury that everyone is different, like clocks can be different. This, he said, holding up the alarm clock, was his "Chris clock." It looked different and sounded different. The mechanism worked differently from other clocks, but told time the same as other clocks do. Chris Chapman looked normal, like the alarm clock, but was different on the inside, where people can't see. This tactic makes no more sense to me now than it did then.

Using a standard "chalk talk" technique, Attorney Thomas pyramided several million dollars in damages on a chalkboard, with the help of the evidence he drew from his hired economist. Unlike his hangdog demeanor after his client's supervisor offered her devastating testimony, Chapman's lawyer was now full of vigor and confidence. He didn't miss the opportunity to describe me as "crass and insensitive" and finished with another reference to the alarm clock.

As I usually did, I erased the chalkboard, beginning my remarks as I did so. I worked the most credible evidence into my theme that the accident didn't measure up to the diagnostic criteria for minor brain damage. Still, if the jury disagreed with us and felt she was indeed brain damaged, the earlier, more severe rollover accident likely caused the plaintiff's symptoms and complaints.

Because I knew from my experience just a few days before that Chapman was a 24-carat liar, I spent some time highlighting the cafeteria supervisor's unbidden blast at Chapman's credibility, hoping my efforts would bolster my own standing with the jury.

I had the awkward and decidedly unique task of commenting on my own credibility:

Ladies and gentlemen, you have a comparison to make. It involves the question of witness bias. Let me tell you what I mean.

Miss Chapman's work supervisor had no axe to grind. She was an independent witness, unlike Christine and her friends and family who testified on her behalf. She was called to the stand by Christine's own lawyer, yet she spoke candidly about Miss Chapman. She said Christine was not credible or trustworthy both before and after the accident. Christine was absent a lot. She described Christine as a poor worker when she did show up.

Christine's supervisor's credibility was unchallenged. She had nothing to gain from false testimony. It seems to me, at least, that you can accept it as absolutely true.

On the other hand, I was a witness too. But I'm very biased. I'm probably the most biased person in this room. Why should anyone believe me?

Here's a thought. If you believe Christine's work supervisor, understand one thing. She and I are singing on the same page. Her experiences with Christine as her work supervisor and my experiences in this courtroom with her have been brought before you under oath for your consideration. It's a simple test. If you believe Christine's supervisor, you can believe me.

Before college, and before women went to work in large numbers, I spent some time as a door-to-door Fuller Brush salesman. The company had wonderful personal care and home products, and I demonstrated some of my favorites to customers out of my sample case. I relied on Fuller's great products to sell themselves, and was fairly successful with that approach. But my supervisor changed my mind. He thought I could do better. He told me to *ask for the sale.* By this he meant, *don't hope for the customer to do what you'd like her to do. Ask her to do it.*

I tried it. It worked. My sales figures went up.

My supervisor's advice served me well as a salesman in college, and I used it as a lawyer. Rather than hope the jury saw things my way I first tried to marshal the facts to lead them to the right conclusion without actually saying so. A conclusion reached on one's own is much stronger and more firmly held than a conclusion demanded by another person.

Arthur Middleton taught me that the best advocates don't try to score debating points in closing argument. Rather, they appeal to the jury's inner voice and sense of fairness, persuading, not cajoling. A good example of this strategy is to start a declarative statement with, "It seems to me, at least..." This phrase gently invites jurors to agree with you, because you are, in a low-key way, encouraging them to arrive at the same conclusion on their own.

Arthur Middleton also understood that a lawyer can't convince everyone on the jury that his cause is right. Instead, his approach in closing argument was to impart the tools of a well-reasoned position to his friends on the jury, who will use them to win over his opponents in deliberations.

In closing, I suggested that the fair and responsible take-away from the credible evidence was a zero verdict for Christine Chapman. I put a big zero on the chalkboard. And I firmly asked them for it.

Unlike awaiting a verdict in a criminal trial, the parties and lawyers usually go home during jury deliberations in civil cases. There's no reason to hang around the courthouse, and, in my case, at least one good reason not to.

I've been present in the courtroom for two of my jury verdicts. You've seen it in the movies. The jury files in. The judge asks the foreperson if the jury has reached a verdict. The foreperson says yes. The foreperson hands the sealed verdict to the bailiff. The bailiff hands it to the clerk. The clerk hands it to the judge. The judge opens the envelope and reads the verdict to himself, making sure it's properly marked, dated and signed. Time stands still. Years of hard work and large sums of money hang in the balance. Then, if all is in order, he reads it aloud.

The suspense is crushing. On both occasions my heart was pounding so much I wasn't sure I could stand the tension. Much better to wait at home or at the office and casually take a phone call from the judge or the bailiff with the news.

By driving home we spared ourselves a long wait, as well as the unbearable anguish of the verdict ritual. The jury deliberated for several hours late into the evening and returned a unanimous verdict of zero dollars for Christine Chapman. Although we had admitted fault in causing the accident, the jury found Miss Chapman had suffered no injuries.

We called Stan Givens, who had listened to the closing arguments in catatonic fear, worrying that he would have to take bankruptcy if a multi-million dollar verdict were entered. He was elated. He said, "I'll bet Mr. Thomas stomped on his Chris clock!" And there was a six-pack of my favorite beer on my porch the next morning, courtesy of my partner.

———

Chemplex and I were to meet again many years following our annexation battle recounted earlier. The corporate brass hadn't lost their displeasure with me, in spite of the fact that the plant was now safely within the loving arms of the city of Clinton and being taxed accordingly. Their low-density polyurethane production was going strong, and was profitable.

A volatile, petroleum-based gas was a by-product of production. The colorless gas had a distinctive and unpleasant aroma. Many felt it killed huge oaks around the area. Indeed, a stately grove of the trees had died, their leafless skeletons reaching skyward for years.

Some of the company's product came out of the manufacturing process in large lumps instead of a desirable white granular substance compressed into such familiar shapes as Styrofoam cups, bead board insulation, and picnic coolers. It would have been too expensive to dispose of the lumpy material, and also costly for Chemplex to develop a system and devote factory floor space to break down the lumps into usable product. Instead, a small businessman set up a facility in nearby Clinton to re-work the lumpy reject. He bought equipment and hired a dozen or so employees to pulverize it into marketable polyurethane. He then sold it back to Chemplex at a small profit. This system worked well for several years.

One cold February morning a huge explosion rocked Clinton. It blew part of the roof off the re-manufacturing plant and badly burned two employees. Twenty year-old Jeff Schultz got the worst of it. He was referred to me almost two years after the blast, when he was substantially healed.

I found Jeff quiet and reserved, even shy. His face wasn't badly burned, but keloid scarring, the bumpy, angry scarring some people are subject to, was present over much of his neck and ears, where his own skin grew back. Jeff thought most of his face was saved from scarring because he instinctively put his hands up, but he wasn't sure. Part of the skin on his neck was grafted, however. Shaving was so rough and painful that he used a women's cream hair remover instead.

Grafted skin on Jeff's arms and hands didn't perspire normally. It was hard for him to stretch his arms. Cold weather was especially painful. Gripping a steering wheel or a hammer was next to impossible. Dusty, hot conditions made him itch terribly. Scratching produced such irritation on his tender, tissue-like skin that he would slap himself instead to relieve the itch.

His grafted skin looked like snakeskin, with small, regular, waffle-like bumps and valleys over the affected areas. Sunburn was a serious setback. Jeff wore long sleeve shirts both to block the sun and to spare others from seeing his appearance.

His recovery in the burn unit at University Hospital in Iowa City was especially painful over the months of his treatment. Burn therapy is so hard on nursing personnel that the burn unit turnover rate is among the highest of all the specialties in the hospital's nursing service.

Burns are treated with "tubbing." The victim is placed in a stainless steel tub of sterile water. Dead flesh is cut off and picked off with a curette and tweezers until the patient feels pain. It's the pain that tells the nurse when live tissue is encountered, and she then moves on to another location.

The volume on a radio in the unit is turned up to muffle the cries of the victims. Analgesics are impossible during tubbing because pain expression is required for the tubbing to work. This often goes on for weeks, with infection fighting, grafting, tubbing, and more grafting.

The state fire marshal investigated the explosion, but the results were inconclusive. Finding a hard reason for the blast was left to us.

Our first theory was that airborne particles had exploded by spontaneous combustion. That possibility was discounted by the fire marshal, and by us. The particles weren't light enough or small enough to float in the air, and ventilation was excellent.

Another possibility was that highly volatile manufacturing gases entrained in the polyurethane had "off-gassed," or released into the atmosphere, and exploded when the material was re-worked by Jeff and his fellow employees. Through testing and further investigation, we settled on this theory as the most likely cause.

But what caused the gas to explode? As far as anyone knew, none of the machines was faulty, and none of the electrical circuitry was defective. Smoking was strictly forbidden, and none of the workers were smokers anyway. There was so much damage that we couldn't prove any defect inherent in the plant, nor could anyone prove the absence of a defect.

But *something* caused the blast. Our expert produced the most viable theory. The epicenter of the explosion was at the end of the processing area above a conveyor belt that carried the re-worked material to large vats. The vats full of finished, marketable pellets were then returned to Chemplex.

The explosion occurred on a cold winter day, when the warmed air in the plant was very dry. All moving objects pick up static electricity, and more so in dry air environments. Our expert theorized that particles in motion along the conveyor belt passing through the dry heated air generated static electricity, causing a spark. The spark ignited highly volatile gas from the manufacturing process at Chemplex.

The petrochemical company was required to make sure the gas was gone from the material before shipping it to the re-work plant. If Chemplex failed in this duty, the company was responsible for the explosion.

Our expert designed and built a model to try to prove his theory. With a different explosive gas and finished pellets from Chemplex, he moved the material along a conveyor belt about twenty feet long in a closed, low humidity environment. A static spark ignited the gas. The explosion blew apart his model but he'd thought ahead and videotaped the experiment.

We felt we'd patched together enough circumstantial information to bring suit against Chemplex for damages on Jeff's behalf. I filed suit in Clinton County District Court.

Chemplex's leadership made no secret of the fact that they remembered exactly who I was. We spent two days inspecting the plant premises and taking depositions. During waits for these events to begin, Chemplex's lawyers relaxed in an air conditioned executive conference room with soft drinks and coffee while I sat on a bench among temporary workers waiting to be hired as replacements if a regular laborer was ill. I didn't mind. Twenty years earlier I'd sat on similar benches waiting to be hired as a replacement day worker at a meat packing plant in Cedar Rapids.

Several discovery depositions produced inconclusive testimony. However, we did gain an understanding of the system Chemplex used to ensure the product was safe before being transported to the rework facility.

The Iowa landscape is dotted with grain elevators. The owners of these massive concrete structures buy and store corn and soybeans for farmers around the state while they wait for a better price for their product. When an elevator is ready to store a farmer's grain it must determine the moisture content. If the moisture level is above a certain point the grain will spoil faster and command a lower price. It's rejected for storage or dried to an acceptable moisture level on the spot.

The elevator's grain buyers use a simple device called a "grain thief" to test for moisture. Basically a hollow tube about four feet long, a grain thief resembles a walking stick with a pointed tip. It has a small opening near the bottom, which can be slid open and closed from the top. In this way a grain buyer can force the grain thief into the middle of a load of grain, slide open the door, and draw a sample of grain for moisture testing. The grain buyer takes samples several times around the load until he's satisfied he has a representative selection of grain to test.

The procedure at Chemplex was to use grain thieves to capture samples of polyurethane from the lumpy product headed for the rework facility and test it. If too much gas was present in the product, it was too "hot" for transfer. The larger lumps were broken apart manually. The gas was given time to escape into the atmosphere. A few hours later the load was tested again as necessary until it was safe.

Upon inspection of the premises it seemed to me that Chemplex had a huge amount of lumpy product requiring re-work. In depositions I learned that there were more personnel who were partially responsible to test for gas than there were grain thieves available. In addition, the employees had several different duties, only one of which was collecting polyurethane for gas content testing.

We got a big break when an employee admitted in his deposition that if no grain thief was available, he would rely on his sense of smell to tell him whether off-gassing was complete or not.

The gas indeed had a distinctive odor in even low concentrations. However, I felt sure the gas in the middle of a load and in the lumpy material would remain long after the gas more exposed to oxygen was gone. After all, use of grain thieves seemed to acknowledge that gas concentrations were higher in the lumps and in the center of a load of re-work product, where the cleansing effect of oxygen couldn't reach it. The gas in the middle of the load would surely release much slower than the gas in the product closest to the surface.

Later, I took the deposition of Chemplex's Product Reject Department Supervisor. The rules of civil procedure allow leading questions of an opposing party, and the supervisor, representing Chemplex, qualified as such. After examining him on the policies and procedures in place, I questioned him substantially as follows:

JDS: You would always use a grain thief to test for volatiles, wouldn't you?

WITNESS: Absolutely.

JDS: And you instructed your employees to test with a grain thief, didn't you?

WITNESS: Yes.

JDS: You would never rely on your nose to tell you when a load was safe to transport or not, would you?

WITNESS: Again, absolutely not. That would be strictly out of bounds.

JDS: Why?

WITNESS: Because the gas in the middle might still be there.

JDS: And in the lumps too, I suppose?

WITNESS: Of course. The lumps too.

JDS: And you couldn't detect it without a grain thief?

WITNESS: Right.

JDS: That wouldn't be safe, would it?

WITNESS: No.

JDS: And an employee testing for gas in the re-work who was just using his nose to tell him whether gas was present would be breaking the rules, right?

WITNESS: He would.

JDS: I had a chance to look at a grain thief here at the plant, and noticed that the tip is brass. Are they all brass?

WITNESS: Yes.

JDS: And the little door that slides open to admit product, that's brass too?

WITNESS: Yes.

JDS: Why is that?

WITNESS: Because brass doesn't create a spark. If the tip or the door strikes metal, it won't make a spark.

JDS: So a spark could explode the gas?

WITNESS: Yes, absolutely.

JDS: I'm curious. Do they come with brass fittings or did Chemplex adapt their grain thieves to their need to prevent sparks?

WITNESS: No, they come that way because dust in grain elevators can cause an explosion from a spark, so they come that way. They suit our needs perfectly also.

The supervisor's testimony and our expert's opinion, coupled with the employee's admission that he didn't always use a grain thief to test for gas, broke the case open. And the supervisor admitted the obvious, that a spark could explode the gas. The company took advantage of a device tipped with brass for the protection of their plant and their employees.

Similarly, while they also had a duty to protect the workers at the remanufacturing plant from the explosive gas, they failed in that duty by shipping a load of product that was too "hot" for the re-work process. The explosive spark came not from metal to metal contact or a short circuit, but from static electricity.

From the depositions and our expert's experiment, it was clear that Chemplex was most likely guilty of failing to ensure that the product was free from gas and safe before it left the plant premises for re-work. An employer is responsible for its employee's negligence, or fault, whenever the employee makes a negligent mistake while acting within the scope of his duties as an employee.

We had discovered a strong circumstantial *prima facie* case for negligence on the part of Chemplex and established the most likely cause and origin of the explosion that maimed Jeff Schultz. A substantial settlement was negotiated on Jeff's behalf.

Unlike some other clients who received large settlements or verdicts and blew the award on a girlfriend, gambling, or other folly in spite of my lectures, Jeff sought sound investment advice and wisely placed his money in conservative mutual funds. He suffers every day of his life. After all these years I'm sure he feels his award wasn't nearly enough to compensate him for a lifetime of pain and disfigurement.

And I've not received any Christmas cards from Chemplex, either.

XIII
COPS

Blessed are the peacemakers, for they shall receive mercy.
-The Beatitudes

Mike Timmons was a well-built young police officer with dark brown, piercing eyes. Soft spoken and polite, he was referred to my office by the city of Walcott's insurance company, which found itself defending a false arrest and excessive force case. Walcott is a small farming community located a short drive west of Davenport.

A year or two before, a Davenport police officer enthusiastically applied his baton to the knee of a citizen participating in a bar fight, breaking it and causing a permanent limp. Predictably, a lawsuit was brought, and Davenport's lawyer found himself on the receiving end of a jury's finding of excessive force on the part of the officer, and a correspondingly large verdict. The jury was so outraged that a generous sum for punitive damages was awarded against the city as well.

Verdicts like that get around, especially in the taverns and coffee shops frequented by my brethren of the bar. Now, it seemed, every minor incident resulted in a suit against the Davenport police force for damages.

Mike was actually a Davenport cop, moonlighting as a sworn Walcott police officer to supplement his income. His clean record, soft-spoken demeanor, and youth work while off duty gave me confidence that maybe I could help.

Mike related a bizarre story. He was shooting radar along a country road entering Walcott from the west. His gun picked up a high rate of speed on a lone vehicle heading his way. Mike stopped the car and called in the license number, lights flashing and an acceptable distance behind the suspect.

While Mike sat waiting for the license tag computer trace, the suspect got out of his car and approached him. A traffic suspect moving away from his car and toward an officer seated in his squad car is highly unusual behavior. An officer's training requires him to get out and meet what must be perceived as a threat. Mike did, and found himself facing an angry man about 6'4" and around 250 pounds.

The suspect demanded to know why he was being stopped, vehemently denied speeding, and moved close enough to Officer Timmons to present a physical challenge posed by the much larger man. Mike turned sideways to put his body between the suspect and his weapon. The suspect nudged him, forcing him backwards.

Mike had no choice. Tiny Walcott had no other officer for backup, and Scott County patrols were many miles away. His training told him what to do. He ordered the motorist to put his hands on the hood of the squad, where he patted him down for weapons. Finding none, he stepped back and told the suspect to turn around. The suspect, now furious, continued to deny speeding. Mike said, "Sir, if you don't calm down, I'll have to arrest you."

The suspect screamed, "Go ahead and arrest me, you _____!"

Mike pulled off his handcuffs, ordered the suspect to turn around again, cuffed him behind his back, and locked him in the squad. He turned off the ignition to the suspect's vehicle, locked it, took the keys, called a tow truck and drove back through Walcott to the Davenport jail. Walcott has no jail and "rents" space from Davenport for the rare arrestee from that conservative farming community.

The lawsuit papers alleged false arrest and excessive force. Mike firmly denied any force at all and told me he was mystified by that claim. The false arrest charge could be explained by the fact that the plaintiff's speeding charge was dismissed on a technicality caused by the prosecutor office, giving the potential plaintiff and his lawyer unjustified encouragement that a dismissed criminal charge would make a civil suit open and shut.

Wrong. An officer isn't required to have perfect judgment in making an arrest, only the reasonable belief that a violation of law has occurred and the arrested party is the violator. Moreover, the suspect had invited the arrest, garnished with an expletive. That count seemed easily defeated.

That left us scratching our heads over Count II. How could the plaintiff claim excessive force when it appeared no force at all took place? The suspect didn't bump his head entering the squad. He didn't fall. Mike had no baton; Walcott didn't provide one.

Discovery provided the answer. The plaintiff was the music teacher at Walcott High School. He was the band director, taught music lessons, and played piano in bars and lounges around the area. He claimed neurological injury to his hands by the cuffs being set too tight around his wrists, cutting off the nerve supply to his hand and finger muscles. His piano playing days were over, and the normal daily activities of life were much more difficult because of his injury.

I took the deposition of his neurologist, who happened to be my next-door neighbor. Fair, honest, and no friend of plaintiffs, the doctor explained that, indeed, objective testing and examination showed severe motor and sensory nerve damage to both hands, which likely was caused by the handcuffs.

I had great faith in Mike Timmons. He was a "by the book" peace officer with not only a social conscience, but also the temperament of a saint. As an example of his attention to detail, during the trial he asked me to follow him to the courthouse restroom on breaks and stand watch while he used the urinal, with his back to the door. He was that kind of cop.

Following up on the neurologist's testimony, I asked Mike if the suspect complained that the cuffs were too tight. He hadn't. I asked him how he applied the cuffs. Mike said he used the "two finger" rule, meaning that he would place two fingers between the suspect's wrist and the cuff, and tighten the cuff until he felt pressure on his finger closest to the cuff. In this way he guaranteed that the cuffs were tight enough, but not too tight.

I interviewed the processing officer at the jail and reviewed the arrest sheet. No complaints of tightness, pain or discomfort of any kind were reflected in the report. While this was helpful, I'd learned not to rely too heavily on the accuracy and completeness of such reports.

In spite of my faith in my neighbor, the neurologist, I decided to get a second opinion. The law allows the defense to have an independent medical examination of a plaintiff claiming injury to provide the defense with a second opinion. If Mike was truthful about the handcuff placement on the suspect's wrists, what else might be to blame for the problem?

Our neurologist, at University Hospital in Iowa City, fully agreed with the plaintiff's physician. Direct nerve compression over a period of time was the only realistic cause.

Nothing is worse than when you predicate your defense on disproving the plaintiff's complaints, and your own medical witness confirms both his symptoms and the likely cause. I started thinking about settlement. Then Mike mentioned something that he didn't think was important at the time, or during our initial conversations. I didn't have to disclose it to the opposition because the rules of discovery didn't require it. Confident of a favorable verdict on the heels of the dismissal of his client's speeding charge, opposing counsel had asked only the most basic written questions and took a cursory, fifteen-minute deposition of Mike Timmons.

The trial date finally arrived. All Walcott taxpayers were automatically excused from the jury panel. As town taxpayers they had a conflict of interest in deciding a case in which Walcott, as well as Officer Timmons, was a defendant.

The Plaintiff's attorney called Mike as an adverse witness. This is usually a good tactic. If the defendant's lawyer is not yet ready, he might waive cross-examination of his own witness until he's prepared his questions for his side of the case, which follows the plaintiff's presentation. He then calls his own client as a witness again and proceeds with his questions.

The best practice is to be prepared to cross-examine your client when the other side calls him on direct. This tactic usually helps turn the tide, or at least neutralizes any adverse testimony at the earliest possible time, as jurors are starting to evaluate the facts and the witnesses. You're also free to ask leading questions of your own witness on cross, while calling him on direct limits the framing of questions considerably. Talking to the jury through the filter of leading questions with your own witness is a powerful but overlooked weapon in the arsenal of the defense lawyer.

I led Mike through the helpful testimony describing plaintiff's aggressive pre-arrest behavior that opposing counsel had conveniently ignored. Then I had him leave the witness stand and put his handcuffs on me behind my back, in full view of the jury, explaining the "two finger method" as he cuffed me.

Still bound like a common criminal, I resumed my seat and asked Mike to resume the stand. The following exchange took place:

JDS: Officer Timmons, did you notice anything unusual about the plaintiff's behavior on the way to jail?

WITNESS: Yes, I did.

JDS: What did you notice?

WITNESS: Well, he kind of scrunched down in the back seat the whole way. His head was almost level with the door window. He was kind of, a little bit sideways on the seat.

JDS: And during this time, where were his hands?

WITNESS: His hands were behind him.

JDS: Because he was still in cuffs, of course?

WITNESS: Correct.

JDS: Why did you keep him in cuffs on the way to the station?

WITNESS: The Walcott squad didn't have a cage. The cuffs were for my protection.

JDS: And given his position scrunched down, as you described, could you see whether he was putting pressure on his wrists with his body weight?

WITNESS: Yes, sir, I believe so, from my observation.

JDS: Like this?

(I sprawled out in my seat, lowering my head to just above the back of the chair, my wrists trapped behind my low back and in contact with the seat.)

WITNESS: Yes sir, from what I could see in the mirror.

JDS: How long did the trip to Davenport take?

WITNESS: About forty minutes.

JDS: How do you know that?

WITNESS: The arrest logs show it, sir.

JDS: That's Exhibit 31?

WITNESS: Yes, sir, I believe so.

JDS: May I approach the witness and get out of these things, Your Honor?

THE COURT: You may, although Mr. Lynch no doubt resists?

MR. LYNCH: I would if I could, Judge.

JDS: Could you unlock my cuffs now? Thanks. I'll hand you what's been marked Defendant's Exhibit 31 and ask you if that's the City's arrest log?

WITNESS: Yes sir, it is, although it says Davenport on it and this was a Walcott arrest.

JDS: And just to save time, that's because Walcott has no arrest sheets of its own, and uses Davenport's forms for its arrests?

WITNESS: Yes, sir.

JDS: We offer Exhibit 31 by stipulation, Your Honor.

THE COURT: Is there a stipulation of admissibility, Mr. Lynch?

MR. LYNCH: There is, Your Honor.

THE COURT: Admitted by stipulation.

JDS: Can you tell how much time elapsed from the time of his arrest until you booked him into Davenport?

WITNESS: He was arrested at 4:16 pm and booked at 5:10 pm.

JDS: Can you estimate how much time passed between the time he was removed from the squad car at the police station and the time he was booked in?

WITNESS: I'd say about ten minutes.

JDS: So taking ten minutes off the time from arrest to his booking into Davenport, he spent about forty-four minutes, give or take, in the squad car with his hands cuffed behind him and scrunched down, as you described, is that right?

WITNESS: Yes, sir, the best I can estimate it.

JDS: And when did you take off his cuffs?

WITNESS: When he stood before the intake officer.

JDS: Does the booking sheet also show his height and weight?

WITNESS: Yes, sir.

JDS: What does it show?

WITNESS: Height, six feet four inches, weight, two hundred and forty-two pounds.

JDS: Thank you. No further questions.

When my neighbor, the neurologist, assumed the witness stand, we both felt a little awkward. He and I had seen each other in our driveways that morning, and we both knew he'd be testifying. I cheerily called over, "Whatever you do, don't confess!" He chuckled and waved.

On cross-exam I noted for the record that we were next-door neighbors, and had a friendly and somewhat social relationship, but were not close friends. His daughter occasionally babysat our two sons. I cautioned him for the benefit of the court and jury that he and I were neighbors. Still, we must treat each other like he was from Mars, and I from Jupiter. The interests of justice demanded nothing less. He said he understood.

Following the usual preliminaries, I asked him a hypothetical question. Hypotheticals are allowed when there's evidence in the record to support the question.

I asked the doctor to assume the truth of Mike Timmons' testimony for a moment. I explained the "two finger" rule and asked him to assume Timmons used it in cuffing the doctor's patient, leaving plenty of room between the cuffs and plaintiff's wrists.

I asked him to further assume that the suspect had scrunched down in the squad car on his way to jail, some fifty-four minutes away, and weighed two hundred forty-two pounds. Allowing ten minutes between the arrival at the station and booking times, the suspect spent about forty-four minutes scrunched down in the rear seat of the squad car, bearing some of his body weight on his cuffed wrists. Within a reasonable degree of neurological certainty, would this be enough time and enough pressure on the nerves of the wrists to cause the condition in his wrists and hands that he has today?

The doctor freely admitted that, assuming the truth of the hypothetical question, the plaintiff's nerve damage in all probability was caused by putting body weight on the cuffs as Officer Timmons described. The pressure had cut off neural electrical activity to his hands on the way to jail over the time it took to reach Davenport from Walcott. The length of time and the assumed pressure against the wrists was enough to create a permanent loss of motor activity in the nerves to the hands.

In closing argument I drew some conclusions from the evidence, as the rules permit:

Walcott is a small farming town, and, like all small towns, word gets around fast. The plaintiff, a well-known high school teacher and director of the high school marching band, was a member of this close-knit community. No doubt he wished to avoid being seen while under arrest. Just as Mike Timmons testified, he assumed as low a profile as possible as the squad car passed through town.

He's a large man. He just didn't change his body position for the rest of the trip. Due to nerve interruption his hands became numb, as though they went to sleep. It stands to reason that perhaps he didn't feel uncomfortable during the ride. The pressure on the three main nerves that serve his hands were compromised not by Mike's behavior, but rather, his own.

The jury returned a defense verdict, sending the plaintiff and his lawyer home with nothing. No appeal was taken.

While I always had a soft spot for police work and represented cops for years, I accepted a single case against them. After Davenport received a lower insurance bid and changed carriers, another law firm represented the city. I was no longer ethically bound to steer clear of claims opposing police interests.

Dennis Rohlf was a gruff, swarthy, bearded, bear of a man who loved living large and behaved accordingly. One autumn night Dennis and a buddy spent the evening at a tavern in north Davenport watching a pay-per-view boxing match. After the match they left for a rural area north of town where Dennis planned to drop off his friend and return home. As he drove among cornfields and barns, blue lights flashed in the rear view mirror.

Dennis pulled over, puzzled that he was being stopped. Suddenly, a uniformed Davenport officer strode alongside the pickup cab at the far edge of the road, assumed a two-handed firing stance, pointed his 9 mm Glock at Dennis and yelled, "BOTH HANDS WHERE I CAN SEE THEM!" Dennis had rolled down the window expecting to talk to the officer, but instead, put his arms out the window. "NOW GET OUT OF THE TRUCK!" the officer barked.

Scared to death, the Glock pointing at his head, Dennis sat still and asked what he was being accused of doing. Without a word, the officer began firing at the bed of the truck from a distance of about twelve feet. Dennis hit the gas and burned rubber, the pop-pop-pop of gunfire ringing in his ears.

Dennis drove as fast as he could down the country road, weaving as he went. He had no idea what was happening, or why. After about two miles his panicked buddy screamed, "Let me out! Let me out!" Dennis turned a corner and slowed, while his buddy, close to hysterical, barreled into a cornfield. He later said he didn't come out for an hour.

Breathing hard, Dennis turned around and crept slowly back to the intersection with his lights off, looking back in the direction he'd come from. The squad car was nowhere to be seen. Incredulous, he drove a roundabout route home and called police. He told the dispatch officer that whatever he was being charged with, he was turning himself in.

The Davenport Police Department had no idea what Dennis was talking about. In a shaky voice tape recorded by the department, Dennis explained he was shot at repeatedly by a person he presumed was a Davenport police officer. The deeply skeptical dispatcher said they had no corresponding report nor any radio contact with the beat officer in the area where Dennis claimed the incident occurred. They suspected a hoax, but Dennis said he would come down to the station in the morning and make a statement. He was too afraid to leave home that night. He dragged his mattress off his bed and slept in the basement.

At the station the next day, the police examined his truck and found fresh bullet holes on the left side panel of the bed and several more in the tailgate. They went to the scene and found confirming evidence that *something* had happened on the remote stretch of blacktop. They measured and took photos of a skid mark. They also photographed a traffic sign downrange with a fresh bullet hole in it and several cartridge casings on the blacktop.

No newspaper coverage of the event and no TV news accounts hit the media. Newsmen listen to police scanners for their leads, but no report of the incident was ever transmitted. It was as if this bizarre event never happened.

Dennis called my office and asked for an appointment. Skeptical, I agreed. After he told me his tale, I was even more skeptical. He took me out to the scene. There was nothing to be found except the eight-foot long peel mark from his left rear tire and the damaged traffic sign.

I spoke to his boxing match buddy, who confirmed the story in all its details. It had taken him most of the night to walk home, staying off the roads whenever possible.

I looked at the truck. It indeed showed unmistakable evidence of being struck by large bore bullets, but I wasn't entirely satisfied. Before accepting the case, I called a friend on the force and asked him about the incident. He reluctantly confirmed what little he knew and volunteered that an internal investigation was being ordered.

Meanwhile, Dennis was in full-blown paranoia. He was afraid to show up for work at his auto repair shop, afraid to go out at night, afraid to go to sleep. When the police are after you shooting real bullets and you've done nothing wrong, who will believe you? There was nothing to do but wait to see what the internal investigation revealed.

The Davenport police department's Internal Investigation Unit (IIU) report was finished in a couple of weeks. Following department policy, I wasn't entitled to see it. I had to sue to get it. I alleged assault, injury to personal property, false arrest, and intentional infliction of emotional distress.

All were valid claims. An assault occurs when one acts to put another in fear of his safety. Battery, on the other hand, is the touching or striking of another without consent. We had assault, but not battery. The officer damaged personal property when he turned the left rear panel and tailgate of Dennis's pickup into a sieve.

False arrest occurs when an individual's freedom of movement is restricted without reasonable cause. Intentional infliction of emotional distress occurs when one is placed in a severely fearful, emotional, or traumatized state without just cause.

The report confirmed the basic facts as Dennis related them to me, but contradicted him on one critical fact. Dennis claimed the officer approached with gun drawn. The officer claimed he drew and fired when Dennis drove off.

The investigation offered no conclusion whether the officer fired first, and Dennis took off in response, or the reverse. Oddly, the IIU had not asked Dennis to produce the truck for detailed inspection as part of the investigation. I wondered why.

I took Dennis and his truck out to the scene once more. The peel mark was still in the road. I had him match the truck's left rear tire to the beginning of the peel mark. I then placed four-foot wooden dowel rods in the bullet holes in the driver's side quarter panel to track the angle of entry. The dowel rods pointed back to a spot lined up with the truck's cab, just as Dennis had described. The bullets' angle of entry and the beginning point of the peel mark left me suspicious, but still uncertain.

A few days later I examined the IIU report again and noticed something in the police photos that wasn't there when I visited the scene with Dennis just two days after the incident and more recently. Spent cartridges were plainly visible in the asphalt roadway, highlighted within circles of iridescent pink spray paint beat officers carry to draw attention to significant features of an investigation. Putting together photos showing the paint, the cartridges and their angle to the peel mark, and knowing the angle of bullet entry, it was clear the officer shot first, and Dennis took off in panic.

Hmmmm. Why hadn't I seen any pink spray paint when I looked at the scene only two days after the incident? Investigators had collected the cartridge casings by then. They'd also taken the photos before the casings were removed. While the paint naturally degrades and disappears over a few weeks, I wondered what was wrong with the story. Was I looking in the wrong place? It stood to reason that the investigating officers would collect the casings themselves after the photos were taken. But the paint?

I went out to the scene again to see if any trace of paint remained. There was only the tire mark on the asphalt, just as before. Not a sign of pink marking paint could be found.

The IIU report confirmed that the officer didn't report the traffic stop or the incident, and that he didn't give chase. But why not? Although a farming area, the stop was several miles inside the city limit. There was no concern about hot pursuit outside Davenport's municipal boundary. The report was silent on that score.

The third shift beat officer in the northwest sector that evening was Tommy Sharpe, a veteran of a dozen or so years on the force. Sharpe had a number of citizen complaints in his personnel file, which we obtained later, but nothing too serious. He was reprimanded for ending a foot chase when he stood a good chance of apprehending a suspect. He hadn't risen far in rank. In his off hours he was an avid motorcyclist, sporting tattoos, a walrus mustache, boots and leather. Cops like Sharpe were known as "cowboys" by their fellow officers and not highly respected.

I was completely flummoxed. There was no bad blood between Sharpe and Dennis. In fact, neither knew the other.

I had friendly contacts in the department. Once I filed suit, communication with opponents without the knowledge of the city attorney wouldn't be ethical. Some weeks later, however, I received a phone call at home one evening from an unidentified source. A male voice told me to check the fire department's call records for the day after the incident.

Huh? What did the fire department have to do with this case? There was no fire and no need for rescue, as far as I knew. I thought it was a prank. I mulled it over for a few days and decided to subpoena the records just in case. The city attorney didn't object.

I was on a "fishing expedition." I couldn't confirm the credibility of my informant. At this point, the city attorney was probably as puzzled as I, maybe more so, because I wasn't required to reveal the source of my information to anyone. As officers of the court, lawyers are empowered to direct the issuance of subpoenas merely on their say-so. A showing of good cause isn't required. Within ten days, I was provided with the record of a few calls from all fire stations in the Davenport district.

Well, well. A DFD fire truck hauled water to the scene from Central Fire Station at the request of Captain Mitchell of the police department. While sworn officers watched, firefighters directed a high-pressure stream of water on the asphalt with their powerful hoses and scrubbed the pink paint off the road where the incident took place.

Plainly, the police department didn't want anyone to see the location of the cartridge casings at a right angle to the truck cab and about six feet forward of the skid mark laid down by Dennis's left rear tire. And all this was done at taxpayers' expense.

I noted that Central Fire Station responded to the call, not one of the outlying stations much nearer the scene. Central is located one block from the police department in downtown Davenport. I suspected that Captain Mitchell had friendly contacts with the fire command at Central, and asked for a big favor in erasing the evidence.

Now it was clear the officer shot first, and Dennis took off in response. And the cops knew it. The police force I'd represented for years, and who deserved my best efforts, had covered up critical findings of their investigation. When the top brass in the department ordered the obliteration of the pink spray painted circles, they couldn't know that a snoopy lawyer would later demand production of their investigation report, which held the keys to the truth.

I took the deposition of the Internal Investigation Unit officer in charge some months later. He claimed under oath that the paint was washed off with a fire hose to discourage curious children from looking at the scene and interfering with traffic. I listened, dumbfounded, poker face firmly intact. I nodded slightly, as though I bought it, and let it go.

Now I was bloody, screaming, out-of-my-mind, hair on fire furious. The IIU's chief investigator, a cop I knew well, expected me to believe the city spent taxpayer dollars to send fire equipment out to a sparsely populated area north of town to make this desolate road safe for wandering children? What children? The school bus didn't stop nearby. There were no houses, just corn and soybean fields.

Non-existent school children were safer with the telltale pink paint removed from the road? Right, and Elvis is alive, well, and working at the hardware store in Eldridge, Iowa.

I was now pretty sure I had something. But what? Dennis was no choirboy, that's for sure, but he had no weapon, and by all accounts made no threatening gestures to the arresting officer or resisted in any way. Although he'd spent the evening in a tavern, the bartender confirmed he drank little and didn't appear intoxicated. Dennis and his buddy left for home as soon as the fight was over. And he had no police record other than as a juvenile many years earlier.

So what really happened? And why? I took Sharpe's deposition. Dennis attended, but was clearly frightened. Sharpe had behaved like a maniac and hated Dennis for no reason we could fathom.

Sharpe appeared for his deposition in street clothes. I required him to be frisked for weapons before he entered the conference room. The city attorney objected strenuously, claiming this was a stunt on my part. He demanded to know who would perform the search. I would. Over many years of representing the police department, I knew how. And he knew me well enough to know I didn't do stunts.

The city attorney was unsatisfied and refused to submit Sharpe to a frisk. We called a judge to resolve the impasse. Once he heard our story, the judge had no trouble ordering the pat-down.

As all cops are, Tommy Sharpe was well prepared and initially testified effectively under oath. He claimed Dennis tried to escape a routine arrest for a traffic violation and squealed his tires, with a second or two passing before the truck gained traction. Sharpe claimed he drew his weapon in response and instinctively shot in an effort to thwart the attempted escape. He was embarrassed by his behavior, and didn't call in the incident.

The IIU report contradicted Sharpe's claim in two ways. First, only the left rear tire had burned rubber, meaning the right rear tire propelled the truck forward instantly when Dennis hit the gas. Sharpe had aimed and fired his already-drawn weapon at least three times before the truck moved an inch. The shots pierced the driver's side panel at an angle before Dennis reacted and stomped on the accelerator.

Worse for Sharpe, drawing and aiming his weapon for a routine traffic stop, let alone firing it in the direction of the motorist, was clearly forbidden under department rules. Deadly force is never allowed against a suspected traffic violator, even one fleeing the scene, unless he's endangering the officer or others.

Second, and tellingly, Sharpe didn't follow procedure by calling in the truck's license plate for identification before the incident. He admitted he didn't follow Dennis after he took off, or notify the department of these bizarre events afterwards.

I didn't adopt an aggressive tone in Sharpe's deposition, preferring to let his cock and bull story stand for the time being. I had objective evidence and much else to contradict most of his testimony. I was more interested in Sharpe's demeanor. Second, I wanted him to commit himself to whatever story he wanted, and then work backwards to see if it made sense.

Dennis sat head down, still as a mouse, listening to every word. He took careful notes in big, block, misspelled third-grader letters. Frightened as he appeared, Dennis seemed as mystified as I.

A week or so later, I stepped back and took a deep breath. I had to admit to myself there was a chance I was too invested in Dennis Rohlf's case to be objective. This ursine giant wasn't exactly my cup of tea, but the mystery surrounding the known events was gnawing and deep in my head. What I knew, or thought I knew, was just too hard to believe.

To try to gain some confidence that Dennis was being truthful with me and not holding anything back, I called him into the office a week later. I told him I was going to give him a dose of truth serum. By that I meant that I was going to subject him to a progressive and intense cross-examination as an example of what he would likely face from the city's attorney at trial.

I said whatever he told me was privileged between attorney and client, and I was bound never to reveal what he said under any circumstances, even a judicial order. If, afterwards he wanted to drop the case, he was free to do so, without charge. He quickly agreed.

Dennis endured a lengthy series of questions built around a theme of skepticism over his story. No other lawyer was present to object to my questions, nor a judge to rule on them. I was tougher on Dennis than I could ever be on anyone under controlled courtroom conditions.

I did my best to squeeze some kind of unguarded candor out of this bear-like man. Failing that, perhaps I could draw out a tell-tale change of vocal quality or maybe averted eyes that might indicate he was hiding something. My working theory was that Dennis and Tommy Sharpe knew each other after all. Perhaps there was some kind of drug deal that went bad between the two of them. Or maybe a dispute over a woman. But despite my best efforts, Dennis passed with flying colors. He gave as good as he got. He even seemed to like it.

For a number of weeks, I was stumped. I knew I had a case, but no motive. Unless I discovered one, the jury could accept Sharpe's version of events, although I didn't think that was likely. But if I was frustrated by the lack of a motive, I was sure the jury would be, too. A jury that can't be provided with all the answers will invent some, and will compromise a verdict when they don't have the full picture.

Using the same story he thought he sold to me at his deposition, Sharpe received a short suspension from the Civil Service Commission. He appealed the ruling to the Davenport City Council. His suspension was sustained, but the vote wasn't unanimous.

I was seriously frustrated. I still had no motive. The antagonist received a slap on the wrist, and no one seemed to care. I felt I could win the trial, but unless I could convey my own outrage to the jury, I was likely to receive a verdict in the amount of damages to Dennis's truck and little else. For a verdict corresponding to the atrocity I was pretty sure happened, I needed a motive, and I needed it badly.

We were going nowhere. The city didn't move to take Dennis' deposition. The opposing attorney's posture was either rope-a-dope, planning to spring into action at the last minute, or he was hunkered down, just absorbing the blows. I couldn't tell.

Some weeks later, another anonymous call came in at the office, just like in the movies. It must have been the same person who called me at home, but I couldn't be sure and didn't recognize the voice. He told me that Sharpe, a married man, was having an affair with a female dispatcher in the department. He suggested I talk to her husband. His name was Terry Marquard.

My earlier telephone tip worked out so well I lost no time in calling Marquard. He agreed to meet with me. Marquard lived in Iowa but ran a small hunting and fishing shop not far from the Mississippi River on the Illinois side. I met him there and was stunned at what I saw.

About the same age as Dennis, with a full beard and long, curly hair, Terry was perhaps forty pounds lighter. But in the darkness of a country road, seated in a pickup truck with only his head and upper torso showing through the window, Dennis could easily be mistaken for Terry Marquard.

Terry locked the door and sat on his bait cooler. He told me he and his wife had been married about five years, and things were rocky from the start. He found out his wife, a Davenport police dispatcher, was having an affair with Tommy Sharpe. He tried to convince her to stop seeing Sharpe, but to no avail.

She promised to stop at least once, but went back to Sharpe a few weeks later. Desperate, Terry contacted the Davenport Police Department for help. He was interviewed at the station by the same veteran IIU officer who conducted the later investigation into the Dennis Rohlf incident.

Fraternizing with fellow officers, especially married ones, was strictly against department policy. Sharpe and the dispatcher were ordered to break off the relationship, and they agreed.

None of this information was contained in the City's IIU file. Sharpe's personnel file, I thought, should confirm Marquard's claim. I moved to produce it. After much legal wrangling, the Court ordered the file produced for inspection and copying.

Sharpe's personnel file confirmed Marquard's accusations, and more. The department's order to Sharpe and his girlfriend to stop seeing each other had just made the pair more clever. They covered their tracks, seeing each other in outlying motels and at Sharpe's house when his wife was at work.

Terry knew what was going on. He called Sharpe at home and threatened him with disclosure several times, without result. He threatened to tell Sharpe's wife about the affair. He told Sharpe he'd visit the IIU officer again.

The affair went on as before. Terry complained again to the department. Interviewed again by the IIU officer, Sharpe adamantly denied keeping up the relationship and claimed Terry was trying to get him fired.

Unfortunately for Sharpe, his girlfriend came clean. Sharpe was demoted one rank, not for continuing the relationship after being ordered to stop, but for lying to the investigator. The dispatcher received a reprimand, which was placed in her personnel file.

Presumably this infuriated Sharpe. He lost his girlfriend, one rank, and the pay differential that went with it. When he saw the man he thought was his nemesis, Terry Marquard, late at night, driving toward a deserted country road, he exploded. If he'd called in the license plate for identification, he would have learned he had the wrong man. *But he couldn't let the department know what he was up to.*

Sharpe thought he recognized his quarry. He impetuously devised a plan on the spot to seriously harm or at least scare a man he was convinced was making his private life miserable, reducing his seniority, and taking salary out of his pocket. To cover his tracks, he couldn't let the station know he'd made the stop. There was no other explanation.

But how had Sharpe seen Dennis before the traffic stop? Dennis remembered he'd seen a squad car stopped for a red light to his left at a well-lighted T-intersection on the north end of a commercial district. His truck passed through the squad's headlights on the way out of town. He was vaguely aware that a car was some distance behind, but paid no attention until he saw flashing lights in his mirror and stopped. Plainly, Sharpe saw who he thought was Terry Marquard in profile in his headlights. He shadowed him out of town until he was far enough away from other traffic, and farmhouses were few and far between.

By now I knew we had all the facts and were substantially ready for trial. After consulting with Dennis, I took an unusual step. I met with the city's attorney and laid out the case for him, holding little back.

I acted for several reasons. First, I held all the cards. Second, while the attorney was in the dark on many of the facts, he and I had worked well together while I represented the police department and the city on other matters. Third, the police department knew everything I knew. If we were going to go to trial, I was losing nothing by placing my cards on the table, face up. Finally, while I had taken a personal liking to Dennis, I suspected that he might not present a very sympathetic appearance to at least some jurors.

I explained my reasoning to Dennis, and he agreed. He understood certain members of the jury pool might not identify well with his lifestyle or be friendly to his claim. If a settlement could be reached, avoiding a trial, so much the better. If not, going to trial would bring this sordid matter to light, and in all likelihood would result in a favorable verdict.

The attorney and I met at City Hall during a major snowstorm. He was skeptical that Marquard and Dennis could be confused. He knew what Dennis looked like, because he'd attended Sharpe's deposition. He had no basis to judge my claim of Marquard's similar features, and I didn't have a photo of him. I told him to put in a call to the IIU investigating officer. He did, on the spot. The phone conversation put an end to that issue.

The IIU officer was caught in the cover up, and he knew it. He admitted everything, right over the phone. He knew personally how easily Dennis and Terry could be confused. He'd interviewed Terry when he was first made aware of Sharpe's affair with the dispatcher, and Terry's later contact with the department. He also interviewed Dennis the day after the incident. The hard truth was that the chief officer entrusted with solving and dealing with internal performance issues for the Davenport law enforcement agency fully and competently investigated the incident. He knew why Sharpe exploded. Then, he conspired with others to cover it up.

Finally, now that my blade was deep in the city's chest and threatening its vital organs, I twisted it a bit. I reminded the attorney of the IIU officer's deposition in which he claimed non-existent school children were being protected by removal of the pink spray paint highlighting the location of Sharpe's spent 9mm cartridges.

I explained how important it was that only one tire burned rubber when Dennis floored the pickup, and not two. I suggested certain fire personnel as well as high-ranking police officers were guilty of obstruction of justice by pressure hosing the highly accusatory pink spray paint at the scene into oblivion.

I reminded him that I'd visited the scenes of dozens of vehicular accidents and a few crime scenes around the city over the years. Not once had any spray paint been removed from city streets, even in densely populated areas. In my view, at least, the cover-up was as outrageous as the crime.

This mess could only get worse for the city, not better. The city's attorney, a red haired, fair-skinned man of Irish background, turned almost as pink as the absent spray paint. The city's defense posture morphed into settlement mode over the next few days.

Although not a hair on Dennis' head was harmed, we negotiated a handsome settlement paid by the city for the conduct of Tommy Sharpe, several command personnel, sworn officers and firefighters. The city's new insurance carrier had denied coverage due to the intentional nature of Sharpe's behavior. The city's taxpayers, including me, paid the bill.

We were asked to sign a confidentiality agreement as a condition of settlement. We refused. Our thinking was that the conduct of the public servants in this fiasco should be exposed to scrutiny, including Tommy Sharpe, the combined efforts of the police department's IIU, at least one command officer, and even the city fire department to conspire in a cover-up.

Heads should have rolled, but didn't. As the old adage goes, in the long run the voters get the public servants they deserve. Still, I'm comforted that at least one anonymous caller with knowledge of what went on had the scruples and courage to come forward and provide critical information when I needed it most.

XIV
Venue

We never stagger, we never fall!
We never lose control of the ball!
        -Notre Dame Fight Song

Lawyers who try cases in rural counties need to understand and account for the local mores, values and customs of the citizens who will compose the juries they select. As one example, Keokuk, Iowa, in the far southeast corner of the state, is a wild and woolly place where tattoos probably outnumber neckties on the order of fifty to one. For another, for many years, Muscatine had the highest rate of venereal disease in the state.

In contrast, in the far northern tier of Iowa counties, Decorah and Estherville are models of propriety and civility. Generally, the farther north I traveled in Iowa, the more conservative were the juries. Whether this is due to the Swedish, German, and Norwegian heritage of the hardy folks in northern Iowa, I don't know.

I do know the soil is vastly richer there, and the populations are proportionately more prosperous and educated. There's a wry saying that if the southernmost tier of Iowa counties were lopped off and given to Missouri, it would improve the average I.Q. in both states.

A wise trial lawyer from out of town will make sure his wristwatch is a Timex, not a Rolex. He'll drive a Buick to the courthouse, not a BMW. He'll buy his trial neckties at Wal-Mart, not Joseph A. Bank. His French cuff monogrammed shirts, fancy shoes and pinkie ring will stay in his closet at home. Above all, he'll not underscore the financial reasons he's in court by referring to his client as "my client," though that's good advice everywhere.

He'll never give cause to the jury to be reminded of the financial and perhaps intellectual canyon that stands between him and them.

He'll call his client Phil, or Jim, or Frank. He'll humanize him at every turn. He'll hold the chair of his female client and the elevator door for everyone without fawning, smiling inappropriately, or calling attention to himself.

He'll evaluate the evidence in his case against the background of the likely make-up of the jury pool. He assumes he's being noticed from the moment he parks his car in the courthouse lot to the moment he leaves at night. He's careful where he chooses to go to dinner and is even more careful to stay out of the local bars. He's a stranger and therefore the subject of much interest among the local population.

If he's in the southernmost tier of counties in either Iowa or Illinois, he'll notice the hint of a southern accent among the locals. They'll notice his more northern-sounding voice. He'll be well advised to make a humorous remark about his "accent" in jury selection to help level the playing field between them.

Is this a Machiavellian strategy designed to fool the jury by making them think you're someone you're not? Yes and no. Yes, in the sense that you want jurors to relax and view you as "one of them" without subjective barriers to communication. No, in the sense that you're simply recognizing and adjusting for two facts of human nature. For one, first impressions are hard to change. Second, outsiders who set themselves apart by dress, language and behavior are often resented, and their arguments more easily rejected.

A client has enough challenges to a successful outcome without his lawyer trying to show how financially successful or how smart he is. Using terms like, "*voir dire*" in place of "jury selection" and "exited the vehicle" instead of "got out of the car" remind jurors that you're different from them.

Unless you're an incurable narcissist, you'll do nothing to hint that you'll go back to a much different home from those most of your jurors live in. You won't give cause to surmise that your family might vacation in Hawaii while they make do with Adventureland in Des Moines. You'll generate no suspicion that your wife might be playing golf at the country club while their spouses are working at the Tractor Supply store out on the highway. Your ego may demand a display of those comparisons, but your duty to your client requires otherwise.

As Professor Harold Hill shouted in *The Music Man*, "Ya gotta know the territory!" Trying a case in Fairfield, the county seat of Jefferson County, the circuit-riding trial lawyer needs to understand the former Presbyterian-affiliated Parsons College located there gave way to Maharishi University, where students take courses on levitation and professors play the sitar. Wishing to remain close to this milieu, scores of alumni have made Fairfield their home. Some have taken the street numbers off their houses and mailboxes in the belief that numbers are evil, driving the postal service crazy. They haven't figured out how to phone each other without using numbers, but no one's said there's any consistency in all this.

If the out of town lawyer is trying a case in Marion County, just sixty miles away, it's helpful to know the predominant ancestral homeland is Holland, with conservative attitudes and views brought over from the old country, handed down and enduring through generations of good Dutch farmers. One sees local pickup trucks with bumper stickers proclaiming, "If You Ain't Dutch, You Ain't Much."

Driving along the back roads of Marion County, you must be prepared to wave hello to almost every motorist you meet. In the charming town of Pella, the local women follow the annual Dutch tradition of sweeping the streets as thousands of tulips peek out of the ground in spring.

Once I came to realize the local legal talent in outlying areas had the inside track during jury selection, I began sending the jury pool list to our local insurance agent a week or so before trial. He could usually give me a thumbnail sketch of not only any given prospective juror, but in many cases, the entire family. I would often caution the agent not to say, "You don't want him on your jury" but rather, just to tell me what he knew, the good, the bad, and the ugly.

I found this practice helpful in jury selection, and felt I was on a more even playing field with my local opponent. However, a case in Burlington, Iowa provides an example where too much local knowledge reached up and bit my local opponent badly.

Burlington is a Mississippi River town in the southeastern part of the state. As with other river towns, it's struggled economically for decades. Many of Burlington's best and brightest have left for more promising prospects elsewhere.

Judge Lowell Kinnett in that district graduated from Notre Dame University. His chambers were bedecked in Notre Dame memorabilia of all kinds, and he could talk Notre Dame sports until the courthouse closed for the day. I later learned that lawyers from Kinnett's district joked that if you wanted a favorable ruling from Judge Kinnett, just enter his chambers whistling the *Notre Dame Fight Song*.

Judge Kinnett's home was in another county in the judicial district in which Burlington is located, so his Notre Dame devotion was something I didn't know before trial. He was "riding the circuit," as all district judges do, assigned for the term to the courthouse in Burlington. I had no previous experience with Judge Kinnett and hadn't asked local contacts about him before trial.

My case had an unusual fact pattern. Mary Beckman was driving down a two-lane highway when she noticed another car tailgating her. The car was too close for comfort and the driver seemed to be pushing Mary to go faster. Mary did, in an effort to put some distance between her and the car behind. The tailgating car just sped up and resumed its former position, just a few feet from Mary's rear bumper.

Mary kept the tailgating car in her rear view mirror, glancing at it perhaps too often. Suddenly, she realized there was a car stopped ahead, waiting to turn left. Too late to apply the brakes, Mary swerved to the right, avoiding a collision. The following car smashed into the rear of the car waiting to turn.

Teresa Taft sued both drivers for whiplash. True, Mary had avoided the accident, but the plaintiff's lawyer felt she hadn't paid proper attention to the road in front of her, and perhaps he was right.

Trial was scheduled about eighteen months after suit was filed. By that time the injured driver was well into her freshman year at Notre Dame. In fact, the trial was scheduled for her Easter break to accommodate her school schedule.

What luck! Imagine my opponent's delight upon learning that Notre Dame alumnus Judge Kinnett was assigned to his case. He had dreams of favorable preliminary rulings, evidentiary rulings, jury instructions, and every other kind of ruling. Of course, he kept me in the dark.

Sure enough, Teresa worked Notre Dame into her testimony several times, including how difficult it is to be admitted to the highly selective university, how overjoyed she was to open her fat envelope and find a letter welcoming her into the freshman class, and how awed and honored she felt to be attending there.

But Teresa's dreams of academic success were in jeopardy. She tearfully described being unable to hold her head up to study late at night because her head ached and her neck hurt from the car wreck. Her first semester grades were marginal. She understood from her doctor that she should heal over time, but she'd seen no progress.

Notre Dame's rigorous scholarly demands were such that she was afraid she couldn't keep up. This depressed Teresa, because she was used to top grades. In fact, she earned straight A's all through high school. Fine. I let the testimony pass.

Teresa's mother testified at a later time, as is commonplace. In what I call, "friends and relations" testimony, she described all the difficulties Teresa had experienced since the accident and innocently mentioned that Teresa got all A's *except one B* throughout high school. I had an idea and waived cross-examination.

During a recess the next day I approached my opponent. I suggested he dismiss Mary from the case and continue the trial against the driver who did the damage. I told him Mary's presence would harm his case much more by requiring her to remain a defendant than she was likely to help him. He could only recover one verdict for damages, after all, and the other driver had ample insurance to cover any judgment against him. After consulting with Teresa and her mother, he politely declined.

Mary proved a smart and spunky witness. She was animated, sure of herself without being overbearing, and scored points on my opponent's cross-examination. Jurors, especially women, could identify with the predicament she found herself in before the emergency.

Catching a party in a lie is like shattering a beautiful but fragile vase. Being human, jurors know that once a lie has been demonstrated, it's hard to believe anything the liar says. This is even more true when the liar is under oath, and has something to lose by telling the truth.

In closing argument, I suggested that Teresa's testimony was exaggerated, having said she received straight A's. Her own mother contradicted her.

An excerpt:

Just think back a few years in your own life for a minute. Teresa couldn't have forgotten that single high school B. Remember when you were in high school? We all knew people like that. If they got a B after earning nothing but A's they'd remember it forever.

So why would Teresa exaggerate something as tiny and unimportant to her case as her claim of a straight A average, while under oath? It seems to me, at least, she might have wanted you to think she is highly qualified to get good grades at Notre Dame, but her injuries are holding her back. That's consistent with her testimony, isn't it? If she'd invent or exaggerate her high school grades, she'd certainly invent or exaggerate really important things, like her pain and discomfort she says she got from the accident. After all, translating her claim of physical problems into a mountain of money is what we're all here to talk about and resolve.

The jury found Mary Beckman free from fault. Teresa received a small verdict against the tailgating driver, consistent with her real injuries.

The Notre Dame references had no effect on Judge Kinnett. Worse, in talking to jurors after the verdict, many on the blue collar jury were put off by Teresa's rather elitist testimony. They agreed she'd either invented or greatly exaggerated her claims of pain and suffering. Their conclusion was reflected in the verdict.

Teresa's lawyer was a friend. Over coffee one morning some months later, he told me he'd also interviewed a couple of jurors to try to find out what was important to their decision. He confirmed that the Notre Dame angle had backfired. He ruefully admitted the connection did no good with Judge Kinnett, either, but it seemed like a heaven-sent strategy at the time. Too late, he understood the effect of what he thought was an insignificant contradiction between Teresa and her mother over Teresa's high school grades. He saw why

I'd urged him to dismiss Mary during trial, but he also understood why I couldn't tell him.

And, he said, it didn't help Teresa that some jurors saw her lip-locked with her boyfriend in the courthouse parking lot during lunch breaks, either.

———————

Mount Pleasant is the county seat of Henry County. Neither especially prosperous nor poverty stricken, the venue is a bland, white bread place to spend a few days in one of the attractive court-house squares that adorn many of Iowa's ninety-nine counties. Mount Pleasant is misnamed twice. It's neither mount nor especially pleas-ant. Its topography generally mimics Iowa's gently rolling farmland, but the friendly, congenial lawyers there make the experience pleas-ant enough. Hank Hallberg's case proved an exception.

Mount Pleasant's great virtue is the annual Old Settlers and Thresher's Reunion. The whole town and surrounding area spring to life in a weeklong festival over the Labor Day holiday, drawing fans of early agricultural equipment, machinery, and farm-related displays of all kinds from all over the United States.

First-rate entertainers like the Beach Boys and the Country Gentlemen are regular attractions. Ancient, creaky steam-powered threshing machines, tractors, and combines, huge iron dinosaurs, belch to life and creep slowly around the show grounds to the applause of fans young and old. The event is probably the biggest yearly finan-cial shot in the arm for the community and the county at large.

The Reunion has a small, salaried full-time staff and relies on hundreds of volunteers for almost all personnel requirements, some-thing that's a source of amazement to the uninitiated. Volunteers from around the Midwest plan their vacations around The Reunion so they can go to Mount Pleasant and work for nothing, not even expense reimbursement, year after year.

Hank Hallberg loved The Reunion, too. For a dozen years or so Hank and his wife, Cathy, spent a week of their vacation travel-ing in their camper to Mount Pleasant from their home in western

Iowa. They operated two of several rubber-tired tourist trains that transport patrons around the sprawling grounds from one show area to another. Hank and Cathy had spent many years volunteering at The Reunion for the sole satisfaction of contributing to the event and enjoying the atmosphere.

A local couple, LuCille and Riley Phelps, visited The Reunion annually as well. LuCille was obese and a victim of a mild case of multiple sclerosis. She was able to walk with canes or a walker, but often managed short distances without assistance.

One evening LuCille and her husband waited to board Hank's train to visit an exhibit on the far side of the grounds. Hank stopped the train at the pick-up point and waited the prescribed two minutes for offloading passengers and loading new riders. He called, "All Aboard!", waited a few seconds and engaged the motor, pulling slowly away from the pick-up point.

At that moment, Hank heard a scream. He stopped immediately and went back to investigate. Toward the end of the train he came upon Mrs. Phelps, sprawled out on the ground with Riley kneeling over her. She'd been boarding the train with one leg on board when Hank started forward. She "did the splits" and fell on the brick platform.

LuCille was taken by ambulance to the Henry County Hospital where she was treated and released. Hank called and offered his apologies over the phone. She graciously accepted. That was the end of the matter, or so he thought.

The deadline for filing personal injury lawsuits in Iowa is two years following an accident. One year and 364 days after she fell, LuCille and Riley Phelps sued Hank and The Old Settlers and Threshers Reunion for damages due, they claimed, to aggravation of LuCille's health problems. Since there was no conflict of interest between Hank and The Reunion, I represented both defendants.

LuCille visited several specialists around the area, including University Hospital in Iowa City for evaluation and treatment of her pain. Although she certainly had pain from her condition before her fall, no source for any worsening of her discomfort could be found.

Believing the injury evidence to be shaky and vulnerable to cross-examination, I elected to forgo my right to have LuCille examined by an independent physician. I'd place the spotlight of my defense on the issue of fault.

I didn't think Hank was negligent. He followed his practice of many years in announcing his intention to leave the station and waiting a decent interval for latecomers to board. Although he could have walked back and inspected the entire train before starting up, I believed that ordinary care didn't require that level of attention. *Could have* isn't the same as *should have*. It's also true that a driver could expect a person to shout, "Wait a minute!" or something similar if they hadn't completed boarding. That didn't happen.

In other words, I evaluated our position as strong on liability and about neutral on damages. In spite of reasonable and ordinary care, accidents will happen, as my first secretary reminded me many years before. While we could be sympathetic to the plaintiffs in their claims of injury, a breach of due care hadn't occurred, and no compensation should be awarded. In a nutshell, that was my trial plan.

Finally, I considered the venue, that is, the location of the trial. Everyone in Henry County knew the value of the Old Settlers and Threshers Reunion to the county economy. Just about every business in the area sponsored an activity or booth. Many residents took part in this uniquely American event and were invested in its success. It was and remains a huge source of local pride and an important contribution to the richness of American agricultural history and culture. I believed that a Henry County jury would have to bend over backwards to find liability in this case.

The trial went well. Hank and others testified that he was following all the rules, and no one else except the plaintiffs and their lawyer seemed to think Hank's behavior was inadequate. LuCille claimed when Hank called and apologized, he said the accident was his fault. Hank firmly denied her story, saying he'd simply said he was sorry she fell, and hoped she wasn't hurt badly.

Then, as sometimes happens, I got a surprise. First, a little background: Iowa provides that before trial begins, the lawyers are required to propose a full set of written instructions to be given to the jury by the Court. The judge reviews the proposed jury instructions during breaks and recesses. He gives those he feels are appropriate to the jury either before or after final arguments, often adding some of his own. The instructions contain statements of the law the jury is required to apply to the facts that in their judgment are most persuasive.

Instructions are critical to a proper framing of the legal and factual issues by the Court. They can be thought of as "marching orders" to the jury. The proposed instructions offered by the two sides to a lawsuit are usually different in important particulars. The judge must sort out the differences and rule on each instruction. If he rules an instruction applies to the case, he gives it. Otherwise not.

The instructions are so important to proper and orderly jury deliberation that there's even a standard instruction that tells the jury they are required to follow the instructions. In fact, although copies of the instructions are distributed to the jury for their use in the jury room, the judge customarily reads the final instructions to the jury at the close of the case to make sure members are exposed to them at least once.

Just before the end of the trial LuCille and Riley's lawyer presented me with an addition to his set of proposed jury instructions. With an accompanying written motion, he asked the judge to determine that the train was a common carrier, similar to a passenger train, airplane, or a city bus.

Common carriers are held to a standard of strict liability for accidents. This means that if the train were held to be a common carrier, my defense of no negligence would be worthless. A common carrier has an absolute duty to transport passengers in safety. A similar analysis is an "implied warranty of safe transport." Under this principle, common carriers implicitly undertake a guarantee, or warranty, that they will safely transport passengers to their destination. Any breach of the warranty is grounds for imposition of damages to an injured passenger, regardless of cause.

If the judge found as a matter of law that the train was a common carrier, the plaintiffs would be required to show only that LuCille was a passenger and that she was injured. The keystone of my defense would be out the window. The only issue for the jury, once they decided she was injured, was how much her injuries were worth.

In spite of the fact that I was out of town counsel, I knew I had the home field advantage, owing to local pride in the Reunion. But if the train was designated a common carrier, taking the case out of negligence and into the realm of liability without fault, I would have to spend much of my argument time trying to minimize the plaintiff's damages.

Not wishing to mix messages, my entire defense was focused on contesting the claim of Hank's fault in causing the accident, with just a sideways glance at opposing damages evidence. Now I was kicking myself for not submitting LuCille to an independent medical evaluation.

I didn't like being blindsided by LuCille's lawyer thrusting a new legal issue into the case at the end of the trial, but had no choice but to do some quick research. Iowa case law on the subject was old, the principle of common carriers being well established and settled. I found the criteria for finding common carrier status was whether there was a defined and predictable route, a defined and predictable schedule, and payment of a fee by the passenger. Finally, the transportation service must be available to the general public.

As we filed into the judge's chambers for the instruction conference, I knew the whole case was on the line. I argued first, there was at least some question that LuCille fit the definition of a "passenger" so that she could claim protection under the law of common carriers. She wasn't yet physically on the train when she fell. She had every intention of becoming a passenger, but was still a pedestrian when she was injured. True, she was engaged in the act of becoming a passenger, but wasn't there yet. If she were a passenger, she would in all likelihood not have fallen. At minimum, this would be a fact issue for the jury to resolve, if the judge allowed the common carrier claim into the case.

The judge didn't think too much of my argument. I wasn't too surprised. I didn't either.

Next, I noted that the law required a defined and predictable route and schedule. I conceded that the train met the route requirement, but fell short on the schedule requirement. It simply picked up and delivered passengers on a constant basis, without any time considerations whatever. When the train showed up at the various pick-up points around the grounds, it showed up. That was that.

Third, I argued the trains were not available to the general public, but rather, a subset of the public who were paying guests of the Reunion. The transportation service was not available to members of the general public unless they were admitted to the grounds for the recreation and entertainment.

Finally, I argued there was no specific fee required of passengers. While the fee for admission to the grounds included the trains, visitors could ride them for free, and as many times as they wished. Some patrons may not have used the trains at all, even though their entrance fees were the same as riders of the trains. I summed up, "Your Honor, this little train is no more a common carrier than the amusement area's merry-go-round."

My opponent argued the fee was included in the price of admission and must have some monetary value, acknowledged my concession that the train followed a defined route, and urged that these facts created a sufficient nexus to create an issue of fact for the jury.

His argument left an opening that hadn't occurred to me before. I replied that while it was certainly true the fee for riding the train was included in the price of admission, there was no evidence presented to support that fact. It just wasn't important enough at the time for either side to take note of it. I took shameless advantage of this technicality, conceding the point for purposes of argument, but not for evidentiary purposes. Since both parties had rested, no further evidence could be introduced. There was no way my opponent could cure this oversight without a formal stipulation from me, and I was not prepared to make one.

I didn't say so, but being knocked off balance at the last minute by a new and novel legal issue made me rather less accommodating to my opponent than I otherwise might have been. Surprise fact issues and contradictions involving witness testimony are fair game in the world of ambush litigation, but legal issues shouldn't be kept in the lawyer's hip pocket for eighteen months and trotted out when his opponent is most vulnerable.

The judge needed time to consider the dispute. He was in his early thirties. He'd recently been elevated to the bench by the governor and was clearly conflicted over this unusual problem. No judge wants to be reversed on appeal, especially a new judge, anxious to establish his authority and reputation with the legal community. He commented somewhat ruefully, "Sometimes I have to remind myself that I asked for this job."

We left his chambers in a fog of uncertainty. Hank, Cathy and I went across the street for a bite to eat. When we returned an hour or so later, the judge was still in his chambers with the door closed. The jury had gathered and obediently filed into the courtroom, expecting to enter the final stretch of this marathon. The judge had told the bailiff he was ready. Then he wasn't ready. His door to his chambers remained closed. The panel was excused for another hour.

We waited. The jury patiently returned from their second recess. Hours passed. Both lawyers knew the outcome almost certainly hinged on the judge's ruling. I re-worked my closing argument to anticipate a ruling against us, just in case. I took a walk around the courthouse square to work off nervous energy.

Finally the judge called us into chambers and announced that he'd decided as a matter of law that our train was not a common carrier. LuCille and Riley's lawyer would have to argue his case on negligence, not strict liability. The proposed common carrier instructions would not be given. The judge didn't seem too sure of himself, but his ruling was final.

Following closing arguments and a reading of the instructions by the court, the jury quickly returned a verdict of no liability against Hank Hallberg and The Old Settlers and Threshers Reunion. Their finding was that Hank had not breached the standard of "due, ordinary and reasonable care." In other words, Hank was not negligent.

An appeal to the Iowa Supreme Court unanimously upheld the judge's ruling over a year later, and our side finally breathed a sigh of relief. I'm sure the young judge did as well. It was the first case involving common carrier law to reach the Iowa Supreme Court in decades.

XV
PENANCE

Since retiring in June, 1999, I've never looked back, until now. I've kept busy providing legal assistance as a volunteer to a county industrial development group, a community betterment organization, two homeowners associations, a golf club, a marina association, a marine museum, and a number of friends and organizations needing legal documents or advice. I've judged law students' moot court competitions and advised lawyers on trial strategy and technique. When asked why I do it, I answer, "Penance!" On the other hand, my somewhat elevated blood pressure has gone back to normal all by itself. I enjoy hiking, fishing, travel, boating, music, and reading.

My sons say I've changed markedly since retiring. Although I tried to shield the family from my everyday cares and challenges, I believe I failed. They say I've gone from an overly serious and stern taskmaster who worked 6½ days a week to a more carefree person with wide ranging interests. I respond that, having shed the burdens of professional responsibility, I've just reverted to being myself. They weren't around before I became a lawyer, after all. The message I take from my sons' comments is that I couldn't balance family life with the demands of a busy practice. The law is indeed a jealous mistress, and more so than even I thought.

Since retiring Janelle and I have sailed our sloop, *Hawkeye*, to the Florida Keys, the Chesapeake Bay, the Exumas, the Dry Tortugas, the Abacos, and Mexico. We've chartered other sailboats in the Virgin Islands, Belize and the Great Lakes.

While living in North Carolina I played trombone and handled the vocals for a New Orleans-style jazz band for six years. We still sing and perform for groups of friends and neighbors around our community in South Carolina. There is indeed life beyond the law.

There's also the distinct and bittersweet feeling that I'm making up for lost time.

When asked if I'd do it all again, I respond without hesitation that I would. I wouldn't mind trying a few more cases, if catching up on required continuing legal education (CLE) weren't prohibitive after so many years. If I were starting over, I'd try, knowing what I know now, to be a more attentive spouse and parent.

I've had it in the back of my mind for some time that I'd like to write for non-lawyers and lawyers alike with an eye toward explaining one man's perspective on civil ligation and the legal system in general. And selfishly, I suppose, there's some measure of catharsis in it. I also hope that in some small way I've kindled a fire of enthusiasm among lawyer-readers for spurning unreasonable settlement offers, trying cases, trying them civilly, and trying them well. I hope non-lawyer readers have gained a deeper understanding of what lawyers are, what they do, and why they do it.

As I've tried to make clear, a well prepared and tried case contributes to justice and advances society by settling disputes the way the founders intended. Without violence or bloodshed, a just resolution reflects the best collective judgment of the fellow citizens of the litigants.

Finally, I hope the prevailing distaste for the law, for lawyers, the litigation process and even the legal system itself has to some small extent been reduced by my efforts here. No other society involves its citizens in the judicial branch of government as much as ours, to our great credit.

It's been an honor to serve my clients, my family, and society as an officer of the court. I've tried to conduct my professional life in such a way that if my name were ever in the newspapers, my family wouldn't ask any uncomfortable questions. Life's much simpler that way.

And I sleep very well indeed.

END

Appendix

(Author's note: I wrote the letter below on a yellow legal pad during depositions in 1982. I put it in my lockbox intending to give it to my sons when they were teenagers. I forgot I'd done it and found it only when I cleaned out my lockbox in Davenport in preparation for our move to North Carolina. It is reproduced here.)

Dear Sons,

As I write this you are only twenty months and seven years old. I am listening to a pathologist who doubles as the Cedar County Medical Examiner. In other states, his job is called Coroner. He is recounting how he was called to the scene of an automobile accident on a country road late on a warm summer night. There he found the bodies of four young men in the burned out shell of a Pontiac Firebird. A photo shows what he says is the body of one of them, hanging out a window. Only an arm is recognizable as part of a human being. The rest looks more like a marshmallow left too long in the flames of a campfire. All were drunk when they died.

The photo shows the car standing in a farm field hundreds of feet from the road, its paint charred and its tires burned off. An investigating officer said the airborne muscle car struck a wooden utility pole after it left the highway, turning it into what he called, "toothpicks." A nearby farmer and his wife heard the boys' final screams, but were helpless to act. The roof of the car was crushed as it rolled over several times. Sitting on its rims, the highest part appears just three feet off the ground. The ash that was a boy trying to escape is wedged between the roof and the passenger door, one arm dangling free.

Minutes before, the young men were having the time of their lives, making the rounds of several area sports bars and a bowling alley. They were drinking beer and brandy, shooting pool and bowling, joshing each other, looking forward to football, girls and school.

The father of one of the boys is here now. He listens, dry eyed, to the clinical analysis given by the doctor. The pathologist explains that his son's jaw was removed so the boy could be identified by dental records. His face was burned away. His father hears how his son's toe was given a tag with the letter "C" on it so his body wouldn't be confused with the others.

The pathologist is nearly overcome. His hand shakes slightly as he holds an autopsy photograph. One of the boys and his family were members of his church. Under gentle questioning by the boy's attorney, the doctor explains how the remains were opened and examined in a cold room in an empirical effort to determine the exact cause of death.

We defense lawyers sit around the conference table, listening with a strange detachment. None of us knew any of the victims or their families. From different viewpoints and with different goals, we are reconstructing the final hours these young men spent on earth. Some day we will all go to court and try to persuade a jury that the fault for the accident lies with one tavern or another. No one can be sure who was driving. No seat belts were fastened. Multiple rolls violently threw the Firebird's precious contents around like paper in a whirlwind.

With twenty-twenty hindsight, we will all admit the boys drank too much. Blood extracted from their young hearts confirms it beyond any doubt. The perfect bodies God gave these young men were made imperfect by alcohol.

The doctor has recovered control now. We listen as he calmly describes how alcohol affected their muscle coordination, judgment, visual acuity, speech and even hearing. We listen to him explain how he systematically took apart each charred body much as you will probably dissect a frog in biology class. Each of the marvelous systems contained in their bodies were examined for minute evidence of trauma.

None of the boys thought his evening would end like that. If they were thinking at all, they might have vaguely imagined soon being home in their beds, and their families in theirs, with no problems worse than the prospect of a morning hangover.

There is a period in the lives of most young men when they are at great risk to the effects of alcohol. When the law says they are mature enough to make their own judgments, many are still too adventuresome and careless. Something within them impels a need to impress their friends and take wild chances. They want badly to be accepted as "one of the guys" and know the security of that acceptance. They long to experience new thrills and take dares. Alcohol helps the process. It makes it easier. It's liquid bravery. Drinking it provides a common ground for them to impress each other and nurture their relationships.

Most get over it in time. Some never do. For reasons that can only be explained by sociologists and psychologists, males pay a price disproportionate to their numbers. I lived through that period in my life, and because I did, you were born. Because I was lucky, you are here to enjoy all that life offers.

My dad never listened to what I am required to listen to today. Dad, probably like most dads, trusted me to use my own judgment. I didn't always. And because I didn't, I had some scary moments. They didn't scare me much then, but they should have. And they do now.

What I'm trying to do is give you the wisdom of experience before you need it. The young men who died in the fireball that gave rise to this lawsuit are the wisest residents of the cemetery. They learned in a flash that young men will always be able to find a tavern that will take their money as long as they have it and are willing to spend it. They learned in a fatal instant lessons many never do, even some who live full lives.

I'm lucky in another way. I've learned some things at the expense and sorrow of others. My words are the poorest substitute for experience, but it's the best I can do. Now, I'll take a deep breath and help your mother raise you right. Some day you'll tell us by your character whether we succeeded.

Love,
Dad

Made in the USA
Lexington, KY
12 January 2014